C000081234

IMAGES OF ENGLAND

CANTERBURY STREETS

AVE ANGLIÆ MATER

IMAGES OF ENGLAND

CANTERBURY STREETS

JANET CAMERON

TEMPUS

Frontispiece: Ancient shield attributed to St Thomas Becket, Archbishop of Canterbury 1162-70. The birds are choughs, 2004.

First published 2005

Tempus Publishing Limited
The Mill, Brimscombe Port,
Stroud, Gloucestershire, GL5 2QG

© Janet Cameron, 2005

The right of Janet Cameron to be identified as the Author of this work
has been asserted in accordance with the Copyrights, Designs
and Patents Act 1988.

All rights reserved. No part of this book may be reprinted or
reproduced or utilised in any form or by any electronic, mechanical
or other means, now known or hereafter invented, including
photocopying and recording, or in any information storage or retrieval
system, without the permission in writing from the Publishers.

British Library Cataloguing in Publication Data.
A catalogue record for this book is available from the British Library.

ISBN 0 7524 3398 9

Typesetting and origination by Tempus Publishing Limited
Printed in Great Britain

Contents

Acknowledgements

The author would like to thank all the kind people who shared their experiences and their connections with Canterbury, helping to make this book possible. Especially the following, in alphabetical order:

Stephen Bax, Richard Chapman, Thelma Cole, Bob Collins, Doris Conroy, Dee Davie, John Durcan, June English, Verna Frisby, Pat and Bill Griffin, Julie Johnson, Lynda and Chris Johnson, David Mason, Michael Patten, Michael Piquet, Peggy Poole, Anne Roche, Michelle Smith, Sally Stace, Kenny Stanton.

Canterbury Library Local Studies Collection, Kent County Council for providing images held in their collection.

The staff of the Canterbury Heritage Museum, the Beaney Institute and the Eastbridge Hospital.

Thank you so much for all your support.

Photographs by Philip Howdle, unless otherwise stated.

Grateful thanks to Katherine Burton and Matilda Pearce at Tempus Publishing for all their help and support while I was writing this book.

Every effort has been made to trace the copyright on the images in this book but the author would like to apologise to anyone who may have been inadvertently left out.

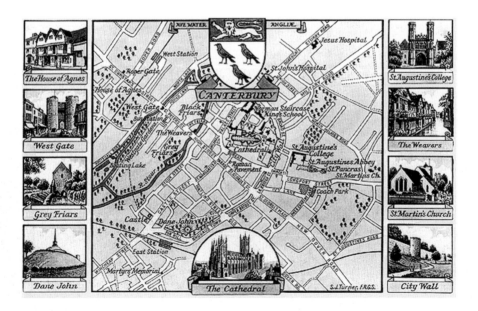

Foreword

This book has been a joy to write and I have loved every minute of it, from tramping Canterbury's colourful streets to deciphering my impossible scribble and transferring it onto the computer screen. I now know Canterbury on many, many levels, thanks to all the warm-hearted Canterbury people who have helped me. While making every effort to ensure the information in this book is as accurate as possible, I hope I am not guilty of any serious errors or omissions. I hope I shall be forgiven for any small ones.

Whether you are talking about politics, buildings, streets or plans, you are really talking about people and how they interact with one another. People are always fascinating and I must admit those I have met in Canterbury are no exception.

Opposite below: Old Canterbury map from the 1950s. *(Copyright Stephen Bax)*
Below: The city from the top of Military Road, 2004.

Introduction

This is a book about Canterbury, about its streets, its people and its recent history. The more I have delved beneath the surface, the more I have discovered about this many-layered city and the riches it offers. The investigation has been a delight and I am pleased to present not only known facts, hopefully arranged in a readable, interesting way, but also some new material. Many of these stories and anecdotes have been provided by Canterbury people who currently reside there, as well as others who, although they have moved away, recall a Canterbury life with affection and nostalgia. It seems that anyone who has ever lived in the city carries with them a sense of close affinity to its streets and its people.

I feel extremely privileged to have been the recipient of so much fascinating detail and also to have the opportunity to set it down for others to share. I hope you will enjoy what you read and that this book helps to show you that the City of Canterbury is so much more than the sum of its parts.

The city from the University of Kent campus, 2004.

The City of Canterbury:
an overview

It's hard to believe that the area occupied by the City of Canterbury was once a swampy wasteland – that is, until our prehistoric ancestors began learning to use tools and implements, finally managing to clear the land and cultivate it for settlement. Prior to Roman occupation, it was occupied by Celtic people of German extraction.

Now, Canterbury's vibrant mix of old and new, coexisting in harmony, earns it a unique place in England's history. Once, Canterbury was a Roman walled city known as Durovernum but around the fifth or sixth century, Durovernum became Cant-wara-byrig, a Saxon name meaning 'the town of the men of Kent'. To this cultural mixture, St Augustine, the Roman monk, brought his teachings in AD 597. In 1011, the Danes sacked and burned Canterbury and killed Archbishop Alphege at Greenwich. A fire destroyed the cathedral in 1067, although, ten years later, the great Archbishop Lanfranc rebuilt it, as well as doing many other good works like building hospitals for lepers and for the aged and infirm.

Archbishop Thomas Becket's falling out with King Henry II is one of Canterbury's most well-known stories. Becket's bloody murder in his own cathedral by four knights on 29 December 1170 was prompted by the King's famous words, 'Who will rid me of this turbulent priest?' The death of St Thomas started a cult, for pilgrims came from all over England and so grew Canterbury's prosperity and importance, in the shape of the many taverns and inns needed to accommodate the visitors. Canterbury suffered again at the hands of a mighty king in 1538, when Henry VIII ordered Thomas Becket's shrine plundered and his bones burned; following this, the monastery was dissolved in 1539. All the jewels and treasures laid at Becket's shrine by his followers were taken away by greedy Henry for the benefit of the Royal Exchequer.

Fine craftsmen from medieval times to the Tudors and Stuarts have left their mark on Canterbury's architecture. However, Canterbury's architecture is seldom what it seems. Makeovers have always been popular, and they are mostly for vanity; for keeping up with fashion and for making impressions. Dating buildings accurately can be difficult, although there are clues to indicate which buildings are wearing a façade and, for the experts, they are as easy to spot as a nylon hairpiece! The emergence of the coaching trade during the late eighteenth century made it imperative to modernise the streets, so, gradually, existing thoroughfares were improved and new streets cut. As always, change demanded sacrifice so all gates were demolished, although Westgate, the city gaol, was spared.

During the nineteenth century, life was difficult for the people of Canterbury, who worked long hours but gained little comfort for their efforts. In 1801, people lived both in the countryside and the town, while farms sometimes employed a number of people who lived in and were catered for by the farmer's wife. However, the price of living was rising, for wheat cost 110s a quarter, more than twice as much as it had cost ten years before; as a result, many parishes were unable to support their widows and orphans and, by the 1890s, more than two-thirds had moved into the town.

The first census took place in 1801 and showed an increase in population of 77 per cent over the previous 100 years. An increased birth rate and falling death rate were having an effect and in Canterbury there were 9,500 people, compared with 10,500 in Chatham, 8,000 in Rochester and only 700 in Orpington.In the later nineteenth century, Canterbury's population had grown to between 18,000 and 20,000, thereby justifying thirteen breweries and a hundred public houses! (Although we should remember that people mainly drank beer as the water was unsafe to drink.) Perhaps surprisingly, the results of the Religious Census on 30 March 1851 revealed that fewer than 40 per cent of Canterbury people were regular churchgoers and that many churches were actually empty.

A further watershed in the history of Canterbury was the Blitz, particularly the raids of 1942, which destroyed many beautiful buildings, from people's homes to fine historical treasures. The so-called Baedeker raids against England's towns and cities were in reprisal for RAF night attacks against German cities and the 1st June 1942 raid on Canterbury was meant to avenge the bomber raid on Cologne on 30 May, an action that destroyed 600 acres of the city.It is estimated that one-fifth of Canterbury was devastated that night during an attack that lasted two hours and thirty minutes. The fire damage was extreme, due to the number of buildings of timber construction, like the weavers' cottages in the High Street.At this time, most buildings in Burgate and Watling Streets were constructed of timber. Fortunately, Canterbury's greatest treasures, like the cathedral, survived thanks to vigilant fire-watchers.The fatalities of the wartime raids are as follows: fifty-five people were killed and forty-nine seriously injured on 1 June 1942, when 130 high explosives and 3,600 firebombs rained down on Canterbury; and the daylight raid on 31 October 1942, when Focke-Wulf fighter bombers dropped bombs and also gunned down people walking the streets, causing the deaths of thirty-three people and seriously injuring forty-nine. The rebuilding of the damaged city, including a new road system, was planned in 1951 under the City Architect, Mr L. Hugh Wilson. These proposals resulted in further controversy as Mr Wilson and the Canterbury Citizens Defence Association battled to uphold their personal concerns, which were those of progress versus the possible destruction of the city's medieval character. The *Kentish Gazette*, strongly in favour of the people, published their letters and opinions, while the mayor, Cllr Jennings, supported Mr Wilson. Eventually, in the 1950s, the city began to change, with new replacing old amid further disputes and wrangling. After all, there is more to progress than simply replacing damaged buildings. Provision had to be made for new technology, for roads and traffic and for a steadily increasing population.

Canterbury currently has a population of around 33,000 and is probably visited by around two million people a year.

Janet Cameron
August 2004

A modern map of Canterbury. *(Copyright Stephen Bax)*

Key

1 The Westgate	19 City Bastions	38 Christ Church University College
2 Canterbury Weavers	20 Tower House (Mayor's Parlour)	39 Chapel of St Pancras
3 Grey Friars	21 St Mary Magdalene Church Tower	40 St Paul's Church
4 Queen Elizabeth's Guest Chamber	22 Marlowe Memorial	41 Site of St Michael's Church
5 Christ Church Gate and Buttermarket	23 Marlowe Theatre	42 Site of St George's Gate
6 Norman Staircase	24 St Thomas Church	43 Site of Convent of Holy Sepulchre
7 St Augustine's Abbey	25 Mercery Lane	44 Dane John
8 East Bridge Hospital	26 Christ Church Priory	45 St Margaret's Church
9 Black Friars	27 Deanery	46 St Mildred's Church
10 St George's Tower	28 King's School	47 Site of Guildhall
11 Sun Hotel (formerly)	29 Mint Yard	48 Site of St Mary Bredin Church
12 Chequers of the Hope (formerly)	30 Old Entrance to Archbishop's Palace	49 Site of St Andrew's Church
13 Poor Priests' Hospital, Buffs Museum	31 St Alphege's Church	50 Site of House of Knights Templar
14 Roman Pavement	32 Site of the Northgate	51 Holy Cross Church
15 Maynard and Cotton's Hospital	33 Site of St Gregory's Priory	52 St Dunstan's Church
16 Norman Castle	34 St Thomas' RC School	53 Roper Gateway
17 St John's Hospital	35 St Gregory's Church	54 Site of St Laurence Priory
18 Sir John Boys' House	36 St Martin's Church	55 St Anselm's Secondary School
	37 Abbot Fyndon's Gate	P Public Car Park

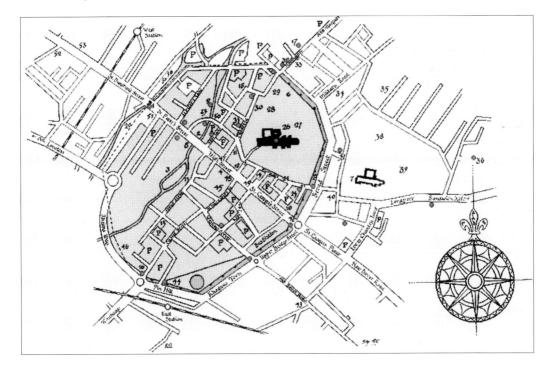

Note on street names and street signs

Street Names

Many of Canterbury's street names indicate its great importance throughout history as a religious centre. The most interesting and historical streets are situated close together in the city centre and are named after saints. As the streets in this book are in alphabetical order, the longest entries are, therefore, grouped together under St. Sometimes, a street adopts the name of a famous person, a landowner or a building: for example, Roper Road and Palace Street. Occasionally, the names suggest a theme, such as military heroes, as in Havelock Street and Gordon Road; while other names are descriptive, like Turnagain Lane – a cul-de-sac – and Lime Kiln Road. The names are passed to the Post Office and then approved by the Public Works Committee of the local council.

Street Signs

Traditional signs were constructed by screwing iron letters to oak boards with rounded corners and by painting them white. They were usually mounted on walls or the sides of buildings, unlike today, when they are often independently mounted on poles.

Many of the streets in this book are contained within the Canterbury Ring Road, and can be found on the map on page 11. However, when reaearching this book, I wanted to uncover some new material including a few interesting stories outside the main ring road. These do include just a few further afield, but within comfortable walking distance for most people. I would respectully suggest an inexpensive street plan, available from most bookshops and newsagents, would add to your enjoyment.

A

Abbots Place

Abbots Place, near King Street, was named after Archbishop Abbott. During the seventeenth century, while out hunting, he distinguished himself by shooting a gamekeeper instead of a deer.

All Saints Lane

All Saints Lane runs towards The Friars from the point where St Peter's Street continues onto King's Bridge. It is, however, a cul-de-sac, containing a fine terrace of Tudor cottages dating from the late fifteenth century and with a jettied first floor. The penultimate doorway leads into the Woodman School of Dancing and it's easy to tell if a lesson is being held by the loud thumping that emanates from the building. (During the 1940s, the Woodman School of Dancing operated in the Foresters Hall in the High Street and, for some years after the Second World War, they used an upper room in Gaywood's Restaurant at No. 41 High Street.) There are attractive timber doors to the Tudor cottages and one has a fascinating carving showing two imp faces.

Cottages in All Saints Lane, 2004.

Above left: Detail from a cottage door in All Saints Lane, 2004.
Above right: Imp faces beside a cottage door in All Saints Lane, 2004.

In 1945, a plan was hatched to solve the bottleneck problem for buses passing each other over the narrow King's Bridge by making a short loop road linking Best Lane and The Friars and bisecting All Saints Lane. Fortunately, the idea was abandoned and the Wilson Road Plan sited a relief road further south, so this tiny, picturesque lane was saved.

Artillery Street

There was a strong community spirit here during the years before the Second World War. Everyone joined in at King George V's Silver Jubilee celebration on 6 May 1935 and a similar fuss was made for the VE celebrations ten years later.

A distinctive building in the street was the White House, which was located at the bottom, near the junction of Artillery Street and Victoria Row. It was demolished in the late 1960s, like other buildings in the area, to make way for redevelopment.

Artillery Street's terraced houses ran along both sides, but the right side, if facing Northgate, was demolished in 1962 and the left side in 1968.

B

Beer Cart Lane

This name is derived from the brewery situated near the corner of the junction of Beer Cart Lane and Stour Street, almost opposite what is now the Heritage Centre or the Poor Priests' Hospital. People drank weakened beer, called small beer, for thirst rather than for social reasons and this practice included children, since beer was safer than the unclean water. The brewery now operates as the Beer Cart Arms and is situated next door to the Church of Christian Science, founded in 1879 by Mary Baker Eddy, which was formerly in Blackfriars Street.

During the 1942 raids, a bomb fell on the corner of Beer Cart Lane and Stour Street, destroying the Weights and Measures Office and damaging gas and water cables, resulting in some areas being without water, a critical loss at such a desperate time.

Several buildings in Beer Cart Lane were sacrificed to plans for redevelopment during the early 1970s. However, the Chaucer Bookshop, at Nos 6-7, occupies a most attractive eighteenth-century building, which was once a private home, but was taken over by the proprietor Sir Robert Sherston-Baker, baronet, in 1956. The Chaucer Bookshop is famous for specialising in rare books.

Best Lane

Best Lane is a turning off the north side of the High Street and takes its name from a local family. Thomas Best was the proprietor of the fifteenth-century Three Tuns Inn on the corner of Castle Street and Watling Street, where Charles II was entertained on his restoration in 1660. Another fine house from the seventeenth century stands at Nos 7-8.

Two businesses were started in Best Lane around the early 1890s. Firstly, there was a carriage-building works at the rear of the Gospel Mission Room in Best Lane, owned by Henry Ellenor, which continued throughout the First World War. A father and son, Francis and Ted Biggs,were employed at the works and, at the end of the Second World War, the cathedral took over the premises for the maintenance and repair of its stained glass (see Blackfriars Sreet). Secondly, a forge at No. 5 Best Lane was owned by Mr George Shilling, who ran the blacksmith's from the period after the First World War until around 1948 and helped to maintain the cathedral's ironwork.

In front of the forge stood No. 5b, an old chapel that belonged to a Brethren society. Later it became the Citizens' Advice Bureau, although for the past seven years has been occupied by Michelle Smith, who runs a fine designer wedding dress shop. Michelle's shop is another lopsided building and, once inside, the out-of-square glass double doors show its acute tilt. Opposite No. 5b is the attractive fourteenth-century building where Michelle originally opened her wedding dress shop in 1991. Unlike many small traders who are suffering from meagre sales in Canterbury, her business has grown and, to gain more space for her gowns, she moved from No. 19 to No. 5b in 1998. Clearly, romance has not gone out of fashion in the city! Number 19 reverted to being a private dwelling.

On the corner of Best Lane and the High Street stood All Saints church, a Regency building of yellow brick, whose construction in 1828 replaced an older medieval church. Eventually, the parish amalgamated with St Alphege and the church was used as a hall. It was demolished in 1937-38 and, in 1952, work began on the construction of a showroom for the South Eastern Gas Board, which was completed in 1953. The shop was set back from the original street lines, in preparation for road widening. The church's small graveyard still exists in Best Lane, although the site of the gas showroom is now occupied by Whittard's Teas and Coffees, with frontages on both Best Lane and the High Street.

Best Lane suffered some damage during the Blitz, including that done to a three-storey building at No. 2.

Blackfriars Street

Blackfriars Street was originally the continuation of Mill Lane. A new Dominican friary was built, surrounded by a stone wall, and since the friars were known by the colour of their habits, the street became known as Blackfriars. The thirteenth-century remains of the old friary can still be seen on an island in the river.

Samuel Caldwell had his stained-glass workshop at No. 28 in the 1930s and his company were employed to make and maintain the cathedral's glass. Samuel Caldwell's son, also called Samuel, continued running the business until he was in his eighties, then, after the Second World War, the business was taken over by the Dean and Chapter of the cathedral.

Blackfriars Street, c. 1910. *(Copyright Canterbury Library Local Studies Collection, Kent County Council)*

The Sugar Boy in The Borough, 2004.

During the 1960s, there was a huge woodyard in Blackfriars Street but the site is now occupied by houses, some of which are owner-occupied, others rented.

The King's School art department is to be found here, named the Cleary Gallery after a rich schoolboy who attended King's. Before reaching the art department, there is a terrace of houses dating from 1836, which has several windows filled in – no doubt to save money when the Victorian tax on windows became law.

Black Griffin Lane

This lane, which is actually a very old passage off St Peter's Street, took its name from the public house on the corner, although it is now named the Hobgoblin and has a fine new sign suspended from its frontage.

The Borough

In 1939, Nos 3-4, were the premises of Mrs Vera Cole's hairdressing salon, Maison Coiffures, and Mr Bert Cole's barber shop next door. People stayed in their jobs in those days: Bert Cole's apprentice, Mr Lou Howard, worked at the shop for forty-eight years, apart from a spell with the Royal Artillery in Burma, finally retiring in 1983. Bert Cole died in 1978 and the family continued to run the business for a number of years. Next door to the barber's was an old baker's shop run by Frank Baylis.

The Festival Mural, The Borough, 2004.

On the blank wall of a building at the beginning of The Borough is the colourful, if now weathered, Festival Mural, created in 1984 by artist John Jones, with the assistance of Adam Taylor and students from the Canterbury College of Art. It was organised by Gateways, with the help of funding from the citizens and businesses of Canterbury and its visitors.

Broad Oak Road

Broad Oak Road was near the junction of St Stephen's and Kingsmead Roads and on one side was a row of cottages called Cotton Mill Row. The cottages were built by James Callaway, a leading producer of fine silk and Canterbury muslin, in 1791 for the workers at the nearby cotton mill, which operated on the Stour's back stream. Times were difficult for the cotton-mill workers, who had to draw their water from a communal water pump located on the opposite bank. The cottages were demolished in the late 1950s and later the road itself was widened.

Broad Street

Despite its name, Broad Street was actually narrow prior to the 1930s. In the early 1930s, Nos 104-109 were demolished to allow for the widening of the road and also to provide the city's first municipal car park.

Before the 1942 bombing, Broad Street contained rows of little cottages on the opposite side of the car park, and the Brewer's Delight public house, a big, square white building. All of the cottages suffered in the 1942 raids, although it was felt that some of these homes could have been saved, as their damage was minor. Broad Street in the late 1940s was a sad sight with the gaps left from the raids, and although the Brewer's Delight continued to operate for many years, it is now closed and boarded up.

Next door to the Brewer's Delight was Walter Hogben of No. 35, who hired marquees and tents and ran a tobacconist's from the 1890s until the First World War. Today, the incumbent is David Mason, who has run World Coins from the site since 1970 – one of only two coin shops in Kent. A genuine enthusiast, David deals internationally, using the Internet to promote his business. Before he moved into the premises, it operated as two businesses, a sweetshop and then a clothes shop. David tells how he found some deeds for the entire building from the nineteenth century – the whole lot was sold for £5!

In the 1950s, the landscape was radically altered. In 1959, Mrs Goldup lived at No. 2 and No. 3 was empty. Beside these two cottages, there were gaps caused by the bombing in 1942. Eventually, in 1960, both cottages were demolished.

A public house, the Exeter, was at No. 57. The licensees in the early 1920s were the Chapmans, with their young son Fred. The Exeter was a free house, which claimed it sold local beers drawn from the wood. The Exeter closed before the Second World War and some time after, the Woodman's Arms in Wincheap gained a new licensee in the person of Mrs Elizabeth Chapman. Nowadays, No. 57 has been freshly painted in white and terracotta and appears to be a private dwelling.

In the spring of 1960, there was a fire in the upper floors of No. 78, the premises of B.W. Cursons, an electronic components manufacturer.

Today, most of the properties here are residences for the King's School.

Burgate

Burgate was originally known as Burgate Street. 'Bur' is derived from borough or burgh, so Burgate means 'the gate to the town or city'. No. 61 was the birthplace of Richard Harris Barham, the clergyman who wrote humorous poetry and stories. He was responsible for the Ingoldsby Legends, written in 1840, which included the ghost story of Nell, who haunts the cathedral precinct known as Dark Entry. (see The Precincts). Barham died on 17 June 1845 at the age of fifty-seven. His son had died earlier that year, which may have lowered the father's resistance because he caught a chill and fell ill at the Queen's opening of the Royal Exchange.

Before the Second World War, the Co-operative Society was at No. 52; Philpot's bookshop sold books, prints and stamps at No. 53; while George Dukes, watchmaker and jeweller, traded from No. 54. A printer, J. Hayes, served the community from No. 55 and J. Moys' General Stores was on the corner of Iron Bar Lane. Unfortunately, Burgate Street suffered badly from Blitz damage and all these businesses were destroyed. The only consolation was, according

The Old House in the former Burgate Street, 1913. *(Copyright Canterbury Library Local Studies Collection, Kent County Council)*

to eyewitnesses, the spectacular uninterrupted views of the cathedral left by the gaping void, which were remarked upon in many reports of the time. St Thomas' church managed to survive the devastation, incurring only minor damage to the windows and pinnacle.

Around 1911, Ernest Geeson moved from his shop at No. 44 Butchery Lane to No. 21c Burgate Street (the White House). Ernest Geeson made sure that everyone noticed his shop: four fingers painted on the first and second storeys pointed downwards towards the shopfront. They said, 'Headgear Geared Right', 'Geeson's For Value', 'Smartly Cut Breeches' and 'Geeson's For Fit'. Further slogans, in bold capitals, abounded: 'Everything A Man Wants', 'Trousers 4s 11d, Smart And Strong' and 'Suits Ready To Wear, 18s 6d, Correct Cut, Today's Designs'. The window was just as crowded as the façade of the building and, what's more, Geeson promised money back if customers weren't satisfied: 'It will pay us to make it satisfactory in every detail; if not, we are the losers – you lose nothing!' The Burgate Street shop was opposite the entrance to the Corn and Hop Exchange in The Longmarket and was bombed in 1942, but by then Ernest Geeson was no longer trading.

At No. 21b, before the Second World War drastically altered the landscape of Burgate Street, the East Kent Model Engineering Co. ran their shop, while the ladies' and gents' tailors, W. Stephenson & Son, operated next door.

Number 20, on the corner of Burgate Street and Iron Bar Lane, was Carver & Staniforth's bookshop. It was destroyed during the bombing of 11 October 1940, and, sadly, the bookshop's owner, Miss Carver, was killed in the raid. Other shops on the north side of Burgate Street destroyed on that day were Lenley's Soft Furnishers at No. 16, C.H. Smith the tailors at No. 17 and Irvine Williams, furrier, at Nos 18-19. Among the nine dead, including Miss Carver, were Mr Irvine Williams, his staff and assistants. Nearby, a two-storey medieval house at No. 23 was occupied by Miss E. Norris's toy shop, which due to the damage incurred, remained vacant throughout the 1940s. Two further victims of the Blitz were the hardware shop, F. Bligh, and the Crown Inn, which stood next to Carver & Staniforth's on the corner of Burgate and Iron Bar Lane.

The part timber-framed premises of Court Brothers Ltd, furnishers, at No. 24 stood on the corner of Burgate Street and Butchery Lane. While other near-neighbours perished, their building was unscathed during the June 1942 raids, but, in January 1955, a fierce fire destroyed the roof and upper two storeys of Court's business, even though fire engines from four different depots, including Canterbury, attended the fire. Court's managed to continue running their business from the ground floor until 1959. A neighbour who escaped the fire was builders' merchant Alfred Oldby at No. 25, although his business was also pulled down in the 1950s by the Dean and Chapter, prior to development.

Another well-known building in Burgate Street was Starrs House, at No. 10a (its opposite side had its address in The Precincts, No. 14d), a Georgian property owned by the Dean and Chapter. After the Blitz, only the cellar and a section of wall remained. Next door to Starrs House was Fisk-Moore, photographers, at No. 10c, who had been bombed out of their previous premises. Miss Laura Barrow, the proprietor of the Little Café, housed in three-storey and two two-storey buildings (Nos 11, 11b and 12), was very proud that all her dishes were home-made.

The Ovendens ran an ironmongery at No. 31 Burgate Street from the 1880s until the late 1950s, selling lawnmowers and garden tools. Their display included galvanised buckets and watering cans hanging from a roof rail to tempt customers.

The north side of Burgate Street was badly damaged during the Blitz and so the Burgate House development began in late 1950, becoming Canterbury city centre's first shopping development after the war. This side of the street was owned by the cathedral's Dean and Chapter, which influenced the architecture of the buildings to embrace an older style, even incorporating dummy chimney stacks. A row of shops, built in a traditional style with funding from the Canadian government, was the first post-war development. David Greig, the grocers, occupied premises on one side of the turning into Iron Bar Lane, while The Maypole Dairy Co. traded from the other side.

The Saracen's Head public house, on the corner of Burgate Street and Lower Bridge Street, was a fine gabled building dating from the late seventeenth century. At that time, the Burgate – the old city gate – still existed adjacent to the Saracen's Head but eventually Burgate Motors Ltd moved into a white-painted building erected on the site of the old gate. In February 1969, the Saracen's Head closed pending demolition, although, from June 1955, MP John Baker White had made clear his wish to save it when the ring road construction was started. At the last moment, Anthony Swaine, architect, added his plea for the pub's conservation, but it was pulled down anyway. Some of its timbers were used by Anthony Swaine to help restore the Eastbridge Hospital, so, at the very least, the remains were put to good use. Later, the Burgate Motors building, next door at No. 71, which was an attractive three-storey construction dating from the early twentieth century, was also demolished. There has been some speculation about whether retaining the Burgate Motors building might have helped preserve evidence from the site of the original Burgate, the Tudor brick-built city gate, on which it stood.

Nowadays, Burgate contains a number of attractive modern shops, including boutiques, salons and jewellery shops, as well as Nos 3-4, which survived the Blitz. The cathedral shop has traded there for around six years, having moved from their former site within the cathedral precincts and now occupying premises formerly used as a cut-price bookshop. Opposite the Edinburgh Woollen Mill at the Buttermarket end of Burgate, on the corner, is the clothing and soft furnishings store, Laura Ashley. This shop stands on the site of the former Burgate bakery, and is very picturesque with its two jettied upper storeys. Its early origins, however, were even more colourful than this, as can be seen in the section on Buttermarket.

Burgate Lane

One of the oldest buildings in Burgate Lane is the Zoar Chapel, situated on the city wall side of the lane. The sign by the door says, 'Zoar Chapel, 1845, Smart and Particular Baptist Chapel', although the building was probably used in some other capacity before the Zoar Baptists took it over. Certainly, in 1801, a cistern to accommodate the city's water supply, having been removed from St George's Gate, utilised the site.

Little was lost to the bombing in Burgate Lane, although a few buildings at the St George's Street end were hit. There was a good variety of buildings, dating from the sixteenth to the nineteenth century, including a row of cottages made of Caen stone that were demolished in the 1950s. Finally, between 1960 and 1974, buildings becoming vacant were demolished and were replaced by the shopping development, although the Zoar Chapel has been preserved.

Butchery Lane

This narrow lane connects Burgate with the main street. Butchery Lane, where excavations revealed Roman remains, was once called Angel Lane, due to the view of the archangel on the cathedral's south-west transept. Another former name was Sunwin's Lane, and even further back it was Clements Lane. However, it has been called Butchery Lane for over 200 years, although there were butchers living here in the fifteenth century. It is as true of Canterbury as elsewhere that certain trades tend to congregate together in a certain area, for example, modern-day estate agents in Castle Street.

In the 1920s, Arthur Bell ran his bookbinding business, the City Bindery, at Nos 3-4 Butchery Lane. He'd started the business at No. 8 St Peter's Grove in the late nineteenth century and, in addition to bookbinding, he also manufactured account books. In the 1970s, the business amalgamated with Canterbury Printers and moved to Hall Place, Harbledown. H.S. Harrison, oyster and lobster merchant, ran his shop at No. 6 Butchery Lane, having started in business in the late 1870s at No. 5 Guildhall Street, and continuing at Butchery Lane until around 1940. Ernest Geeson, tailor, traded from No. 44 Butchery Lane until around 1910 when he moved his premises to Burgate Street.

Peggy Poole tells how, during the 1942 Blitz, incendiary bombs set the area ablaze. The fire was heading down towards Butchery Lane when the wind changed direction and blew the flames back on themselves. Butchery Lane was then known as the street where everything was old on one side and new on the other. 'I did request that the Civic Society put a plaque up to this effect, but nothing was done,' she says.

Shops on the east side of Butchery Lane that survived the Blitz included Court & Cooke, electrical engineers at No. 15, a fairly modern shop dating from the 1930s. The shops next door to Court & Cooke were Brighter Homes at No. 14 and F.W. Finnis, bakers at No. 13. These once had timber-framed upper storeys but, although they survived the Blitz, they were removed in the 1950s. The upper storeys of Court & Cooke were damaged in a fire in January 1955 and had to be demolished but the business continued to trade from the ground floor until 1959. The remains of the shop were demolished in July 1959 because they backed on to the Longmarket site, which was due for redevelopment. Number 16 was a jettied timber-framed building, part of Court Bros Ltd, as was a larger building on the opposite side of the street.

After the war, Burton Montague Ltd, an impressive shop on the corner of the east side of Butchery Lane and The Parade, also continued to operate with its upper storeys removed. Between Burton Montague Ltd and the remainder of the east side, a row of four prefabricated shops was erected, while the Midland Bank stood on the opposite, west side, corner of Butchery Lane and The Parade.

The Canterbury Roman Museum in Butchery Lane may also interest the visitor, as it takes them on a journey through Roman Canterbury, showing the progress of archaeologists when excavating the Longmarket shopping centre. There are displays of Roman artefacts, scenes from everyday life and computer simulations to show how the Roman houses looked.

Buttermarket

Two hundred years ago, Buttermarket was called the Bullstake. Here, in the special bullring, bulls were baited prior to slaughter. Bull-baiting was a popular medieval sport. It was also believed that the distress of the animal tenderised its meat and, after the baiting, the animals were moved on to Butchery Lane to be slaughtered.

The idea of the Buttermarket was to provide an open-sided building in which local farmers could trade their wares. After the original building was taken down, it was replaced

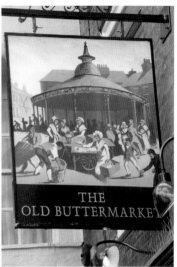

Above left: The modern Buttermarket, May 2004.
Above right: Inn sign for The Old Buttermarket, 2004.

by a more substantial edifice, although this was later replaced by the war memorial, which stands in a prominent position outside the Christ Church gateway in this irregularly-shaped square. One of the names on the war memorial is that of Philip Thornton, whose moving story is told in the section on Stone Street. The Christ Church gateway was built in 1517 and there is a stunning image of Christ above its pedestrian walkway.

On the east side of the Buttermarket is a fifteenth-century building, formerly the Bull Inn, built by the cathedral to accommodate poor pilgrims visiting the shrine of Thomas Becket. The inn was built with three jettied ranges, one facing the Buttermarket, one facing Burgate Street and another facing Butchery Lane, with shops on the ground floor and lodgings above. Around 1517, the Christ Church gate was added, with a porter's lodge to the left, a jettied timber building whose remains are still apparent today. Previously, The Bull or The White Bull was the name of a large house built of stone near the priory in the twelfth century, whose rent in 1370 was recorded as being twenty pence. Nowadays, Laura Ashley occupies the site.

The public house called the Old Buttermarket was actually built as an infill between two medieval buildings, one of which was the bullring. This inn was once used by a Mr Walker as a wine and spirit store and became a public house in the early twentieth century. Originally, it was known as the Olive Tree – some of the older clients still use this name – and during the 1990s it was named the Franklin and Firkin after the character in Chaucer's *Canterbury Tales*. With the assistance of Canterbury City Council, it underwent some restoration in 2001.

Three busy streets converge at the Buttermarket: Sun Street, Mercery Lane and Burgate, making it a meeting place for both locals and tourists. There is an incongruous mixture of styles, with the imposing grandeur of the Christ Church gateway juxtaposed with the Starbucks café next door. Modern shops span both sides of the Mercery Lane entrance – Debenhams café is on one side and Monsoon on the other. Monsoon's site was previously a china reject shop and before that it was Morelli's café. Around thirty years ago, Cullen's grocers, remembered for the fine tins of biscuits on display, occupied this prime site. During the twentieth century, Buttermarket was known for two high-class grocers: Theobald's and Cooper's.

One of the Buttermarket's longest-established residents is Richard Chapman, a family man, who has run the pottery shop for forty years. Richard's mother, Elizabeth, was herself a potter and took over the shop in 1963, and Richard says that there was never any doubt that he would follow in her footsteps. He attended the King's School as a boy and first learned to throw pots in class. He recalls that when he first joined King's, there was only one girl in attendance, in the sixth form. Today, the entire school is co-educational. Richard enjoyed his schooldays, getting up to the usual boys' scrapes and seeing how far he could go. Punishment was usually lines, or being made to run around the Green Court. Richard's shop attracts regular clients, both locally and from abroad, and all of the goods are produced on the premises in his small workshop at the back, including pots, teapots, wine barrels, place signs, wall hangings and money-boxes.

Below: The Canterbury Pottery shop in the Buttermarket, 2004.
Below right: Potter Richard Chapman at work, 2004.

C

Canterbury Lane

Canterbury Lane lies to the east of St Thomas' Roman Catholic church and, after the Blitz, most of St George's primary school still stood on the east side of the lane.

Number 10 was the Society of Friends Meeting House, which opened in March 1688, but this building was devastated in the Blitz. The Meeting House had been improved considerably during its lifetime and its custodians were proud to relate how, during 1772, permanent seats were installed on each side, with space in the middle, to accommodate 100 people.

In 1928, the machine bakery was built in Canterbury Lane from virtually bombproof concrete. Operated by Nicholas Kingsman Ltd, the bakery survived the Blitz but succumbed to progress when, around 1953, redevelopment in surrounding areas meant the business had to be destroyed for road-widening and new shops.

During the Blitz, Jack Walker, a bus driver, lived in Canterbury Lane. A late shift on the buses meant that he arrived home around 5.00 a.m. When the air-raid warning went off, instead of going down to the cellar, the Walkers decided they would be safer in the solidly built Lloyns bakery, next door. So they went into the bakery and, sure enough, their house was hit by an incendiary bomb. Opposite the bakery lived a Mrs Barwick and another lady, possibly her sister, and a soldier with his girl.

Castle Street

Castle Street is a mixture of the commercial and the domestic. It was named after the Norman castle standing on a platform of rubble and Roman brick within the city wall. Originally, the castle was sited on top of the Dane John but it was moved to its present position in 1095. In the Middle Ages, the keep became a prison for east Kent. The captives, although chained, were permitted to beg for money and food from passers-by and some actually managed to break free and flee to safety abroad. Other prisoners had a tougher time and those persecuted by Queen Mary were incarcerated and burnt at the stake. In 1792, the castle's ditch was filled in and the surrounding walls demolished.

William Somner, who wrote *Antiquities of Canterbury* in 1640, was born at No. 5 and attended King's School. The book was published at the onset of the Civil War and the Cromwellian forces made good use of its contents by using the information it contained to gain access t the city. As a result, Somner was later imprisoned for anti-parliamentary activities.

In the 1820s, the Gas Light Coke & Water Co. bought the castle, thereby causing damage to the interior from machinery and coal. Around the 1920s, it was still housing coal in its keep for the nearby Canterbury gasworks at the top of Castle Street. During the last years of the war, a common sight was an East Kent bus outside the works being refuelled with coal gas, an alternative to the newly rationed petrol. The buses were specially adapted and carried the gas in a bag on the roof, although it was reported that sometimes the bags blew away in the wind. Redundant Victorian gaswork buildings were demolished in 1960 although the office of the Canterbury & District Water Co. remained. Later, the land was purchased by Canterbury City Council and all remaining buildings and the gasometer, which was visible for miles but long redundant, were demolished to provide space for a temporary car park. The castle itself was taken over in 1928 by the council, who restored it to its present condition. It was opened to the public in 1997.

During the nineteenth century, No. 49 was a butcher's shop and No. 50 a baker's. In fact, there were three bakers in Castle Street during the late nineteenth century, including one at No. 70 because bread was baked on the premises and was the staple diet of the people. Numbers 53-55 dated from the seventeenth century, although they were later re-fronted and then converted into shops. In 1882, No. 53 housed labourer Matthew Weed and Mrs Lansfield, a washerwoman, plied her trade at No. 54, while, next door, the greengrocer's at No. 55 was run by Mrs Comford. Miss Hearnden and Mrs Goldup, both dressmakers, occupied No. 56 and, at No. 57, George Cole traded as a plumber and painter. No. 58 belonged to a carpenter, James Hookway, Number 59 to a plumber, Alfred Street and No. 60 to a Mrs Ford, who was a laundress and a shopkeeper. Mrs Davies lived at No. 61, while a coachman, Stephen Pitcher, lived at No. 63.

In the early twentieth century, No. 65 was a grocer's and pork butcher's, while, at No. 66, a fried-fish shop traded for around sixty years. There was also a newsagent and general stores and a sub-post office. At No. 67 an inn known as the Black Dog was built in 1692 and closed in 1975. The innkeeper in 1792 was John Tivelan and, in 1882, a Mr Thomas Marsh took over, but the site is now occupied by a gold- and silversmith. Solicitors Mowll & Mowll occupied No. 68 for over 100 years, while No. 77, originally a corn and fodder

Castle Street, 2004.

store, was taken over by Court Brothers' ironmongers. Baker William Thomlow lived at No. 80 in 1847 with his two apprentices and two female servants. These premises also became occupied by solicitors before becoming the Canterbury District Register Office. Numbers 81-82 were occupied by Geering & Collyer, Estate Agents but in the mid-nineteenth century were a boarding school for boys, whose proprietor was a Mary Morris. In 1920, there was a bootmaker at No. 81 and Whitworth & Green, cycle-makers, occupied No. 82, while a number of other properties in this area were owned by the Lavender family.

The Castle Hotel was at No. 30, at the junction with Wincheap Green. It attracted many colourful local characters, such as Drummer Jack, who was a drummer in the 3rd Battalion of the Buffs. In the late 1920s, the licensee was Edward Leavers. This fine Tudor-style hotel was demolished in 1963 for the construction of the Wincheap roundabout, which merges traffic from Wincheap and the inner city road.

Between June 1942 and December 1957, No.1 Castle Street housed Sun Insurance, made homeless after their former offices in St George's Lane were destroyed in the bombing. (The new Sun Building was erected on the same site as the original construction and was ready for re-occupation in 1957.)

Secodi Music, who came here from The Friars in June 1996, occupies a large white building in Castle Street, while at the end of Castle Street stands the Three Tuns public house, which occupies the site of a large amphitheatre from Roman times.

The Causeway

The Causeway, once notorious for flooding, was raised to provide a pathway over swampy ground. Now the river is diverted through man-made channels and regulated further upstream. A windmill used to stand on the corner of the Causeway and St Stephen's Road but a fire destroyed its central timbers in 1954 and it was dismantled in July 1958 for the construction of a road junction. The retirement flats standing on the site in a slightly reduced space mimic its style.

Chaucer Road

Chaucer Road, which takes its name from Canterbury's most famous son, was entirely taken up with army barracks, which stretched from Old Park Avenue to Sturry Road. Most of Chaucer Road is now taken over by civic buildings, with the civic centre on the left and the law courts on the right. The road then rises up, through a residential area with a few modern properties, towards the MOD training centre.

Church Street St Paul's

A most attractive building in Church Street St Paul's is the eleventh-century building with its projecting upper storey, which was used as a tea room in the 1950s. Previously, the building was owned by James Long & Co. but was taken over by A & D Rose.

Cossington Road

Cossington Road starts at Oaten Hill, executes a ninety-degree turn and runs into the Old Dover Road, where the Phoenix public house stands on the corner. Small Victorian terraces predominate at the Oaten Hill end, although the houses become more modern towards the Old Dover Road junction.

Thelma Cole's family took two rooms at No. 21 when they moved from Nonnington to Canterbury in 1942. In 1943, the house next door, No. 22, became available for rent and the family moved in. Thelma had a sister, Lynetta, and two brothers, one in the RAF, the other in the army. The boys eventually found council accommodation, one moving into a prefab in Downs Road while the other went to the London Road estate. Thelma's mother, Kathleen, died of a heart attack at the house in 1951 and her father, Richard, of a stroke in 1963. Lynetta moved away to get married, then Thelma married for the second time, finally moving away in 1977, which was a wrench, as the family had lived in the house for thirty-four years.

Sisters Ruth and Margaret Taylor, aged twenty-seven and seventeen respectively, lived at Cossington House. Ruth worked at the Royal Insurance Co. and Margaret at the Municipal Offices, but Ruth doubled up as a part-time ambulance driver. During one of the wartime bombing raids, they were under a table with their mother, father, younger sister Barbara and a friend with a six-month-old baby. There was a terrible noise of planes, falling bombs

Richard, Kathleen, Thelma and Lynetta Cole at No. 22 Cossington Road in the 1940s. *(Courtesy of Thelma Cole)*

and explosions and, as the noise abated, the family surfaced to find all their windows gone and the area in chaos, with neighbouring homes burning. While Ruth went off to report for ambulance duty, the other women helped homeless people seeking shelter. When Ruth arrived home from ambulance duty, she found every room occupied by sleeping children, refugees from the devastation in Cossington Road. Mr Taylor's shop was destroyed, as was his store in Ivy Lane and all of his records, kept in the safe, were burned.

Cow Lane

A man called Smith used this lane for driving his cows to the dairy opposite the Hop Poles public house at the top, where he milked them then fetched them back. In those days, animals had precedence and the traffic had to stop for Mr Smith to conduct his livelihood.

D

Dover Street

During Saxon times, Dover Street was a cattle market and that is what its original name, Ritherchiape or Rethercheap, means. The name was changed at the end of the fifteenth century to Dover Lane and, in 1870, Dover Lane became Dover Street. Sometimes it was still called Market Way, since animals were still driven along to the cattle market.

A market has been in existence near the city wall, opposite the end of Dover Street, since medieval times. (A cattle market had been held in Canterbury for 1000 years immediately outside the city walls between the Ridingate and St George's Gate.) During the 1930s, fêtes were held there to raise money for the new Kent and Canterbury Hospital and horse-trading by gypsies was still highly active at the site in 1946. The cattle market was moved to a new site in 1955, due to the construction of the ring road, and the former market area became a car park used by patrons of the Regal cinema.

The Flying Horse Inn occupies the corner of Dover Street and Upper Bridge Street and dates from 1574. It has a colourful and well-documented history, originally being part of the estate of Thomas Fayrechilde, merchant. It passed through the Fayrechilde family until Elizabeth bequeathed it to her friend, Elizabeth Sparrowe, in 1672, and she, in turn, leased it to her son George, who named it The Three Musketeers. The pub continued to change hands, gaining in popularity, although there was a blip in 1789 when one Thomas Lechard was fined 10s for allowing gambling on the premises! It was owned during the 1930s by Fremlin's brewery and was also run for a while under the Rigden's umbrella. Now it is a Whitbread pub, whose friendly young manager, Charles McCabe, has successfully operated here for the past three years.

There was once an oast house in Dover Street, which was originally built in 1811. By the end of 1959, the oast house had been demolished and the site was then occupied by the rear extension to the Martin Walters Garage, whose frontage occupied St George's Place. Simultaneously, old houses on the south side of Dover Street were pulled down to accommodate a new garage and petrol station, Bligh Bros. This garage was pulled down to enable the development of a new office block, although it was never completed and the site became a car park. The Netto supermarket now occupies the Martin Walters site.

During the late nineteenth century, No. 2 was occupied by Albert Neame, a woodturner, and No. 3 was a greengrocer's owned by a Mr and Mrs Tuff. Then the premises changed hands and Percy Parsons ran his tobacconist's shop with the help of his wife, and the business continued until the late 1960s, while Edward Carr owned the newsagent's at No. 4. Today, a Thai restaurant trades at No. 1, then there is another, double-fronted restaurant, while the new occupiers of No. 3 are Angela and Kevin Bradshaw. Angela and Kevin moved in during September 2003, having taken over from an Italian couple, A & A Caggiano, who had occupied the shop for seventeen years. Angela says No. 3 is the oldest building in the street.

The Flying Horse on the corner of Dover Street.

Above: The Duck Lane sign – but the name has nothing to do with ducks – 2004.

Right: The Duck Lane antique shop, formerly a coaching inn, 2004.

A lady called Daisy Goldsock lived with her cat, Felix, in one of the old cottages. Daisy was a Salvationist and often accompanied her young friend, Thelma Cole, to open-air meetings. Thelma says: 'If you ever said "Bye, take care" to her, she would say, "If they pick me up in the dark, they'll put me down in the light"'. Daisy's cottage was knocked down after the war and, today, Connexions have their office site there.

Duck Lane

Duck Lane is fairly close to the river although with the St Radigund's car park separating it from the water, people might think it is probably too built-up to be attractive to ducks these days. The people who live in the lane are obviously attached to the duck image, since a colourful tin duck is fixed above the street sign. However, the idea that Duck Lane was named for this colourful waterbird is a fallacy. In fact, the word Duck is derived from the sound of a word contained in a Latin phrase meaning 'leading to the river' (*ducere* – to lead), and that is exactly what Duck Lane does – today, via the car park.

One side contains a row of cottages from the early twentieth century, although, on the other side, the cottages look somewhat newer. All continue the water theme in their housenames: No. 4 is Frog Cottage, No. 5 is Beak Cottage, No. 8 is Tadpole Cottage and No. 16 is Pond House. Number 6 departs from the theme with its name, Hope Cottage. A tiny timber-framed antique shop, painted black and crammed with treasures, snuggles between No. 2 and No. 3. This is the Coach House, and was, as its name implies, originally a coach house.

F

The Friars

The Marlowe Theatre, which stands in The Friars, was a former cinema. In the 1930s, a fierce competition arose between two entrepreneurs to provide Canterbury with a smart modern cinema, so Charles Donada (County Cinema) and Oscar Deutsch (Odeon Cinema) both opened a new cinema on 5 August 1933. The Friars theatre was one, while a short distance away was the Odeon Hall. The profits of these pre-war cinemas rose steeply as people flocked to see the shows, not only moving pictures but also other events such as the Miss Canterbury competition. During the Second World War, the veranda of The Friars theatre was used as a lookout post, while the Air Training Corps used the cellar. In 1955, the Friars theatre became the Odeon cinema. It featured children's Saturday Morning Cinema, until 1978. One of the last shows at the Odeon featured a performance from the pop star David Essex on 5 October 1981. After this, the Odeon was left unused but finally the city council agreed to the purchase of the Odeon as the new Marlowe Theatre, which opened, much improved, on 27 September 1984, in the presence of the Duke of Kent. The new theatre cost almost £2.75million.

Below: The Marlowe Theatre in the Friars.

Today missionaries still visit Canterbury. These two, in The Friars, are from the United States, 2004.

The Mitre Inn has stood at No. 12 since around 1800, although it has been known as the Canterbury Tales since 1981. Now it is used by theatre patrons as well as regulars. During the 1940s, next door to the inn was an ironmonger's called Field & Jordan but the premises were demolished some time ago.

The plot at Nos 4-5 was occupied by Friars Garage Ltd prior to 1949, then it was converted into the San Maria restaurant, and today, once again, it is a garage showroom. The family-run Pilgrims Hotel is at No. 18.

G

Gas Street

Gas Street was a tiny alley blighted by pollution from the gasworks, a deprived area often described as a slum. Yet people remember the proud local housewives who sported snowy-white aprons. The tragic truth shown by the 1841 census is that unsanitary and overcrowded conditions caused death at an average age of thirty-four.

Giles Lane

North of the city lies the University of Kent complex, dissected by Giles Lane. The original occupiers of the site were Brotherhood and Beverley farms. Beverley farm was a mixture of medieval and Victorian construction. From the university campus, on the grassy slopes beside Giles Lane, is a magnificent view of Canterbury surrounding its cathedral, the heart of the Anglican community in England. This raised area was used as a vantage point during the war by people fascinated by the spectacular flares and brilliant cascades of lights illuminating Canterbury on the night of the 1942 raid. One account records that 100 people watched the terrible destruction, including the toppling of church steeples, a spectacle that was frequently described as beautiful.

While the university was being established, the farmhouse was used as an administrative centre. Its derelict outbuildings and barn were destroyed to allow construction to begin on the modernist buildings that form the campus and, in October 1965, the first undergraduates were accepted at the university.

With the arrival of the university, Canterbury gained a new theatre and cinema, sited next to the Cornwallis building and opposite the large car park in Giles Lane. Opened in October 1969, it was originally known as the Canterbury Film Theatre but later became Cinema 3 (deferring to the larger ABC and the Odeon). It is now called the Gulbenkian, in honour

The Templeman Library at the University of Kent, 2004.

A new complex being built on the St Stephen's Hill boundary as Phase 2 of the Tyler Project, May 2004.

of the great philanthropist, Calouste Sarkis Gulbenkian (1869-1955), a Turkish-born oil magnate and the first businessman to exploit Iraqi oilfields. He bequeathed his large fortune to the Calouste Gulbenkian Foundation to help social and cultural projects around the world. The Gulbenkian theatre seats around 300 people.

Gordon Road

Gordon Road in Wincheap is one of many roads across the country named after General Gordon, who was posthumously honoured for holding out for 117 days in the Siege of Khartoum in 1885. Gordon Road once contained East station, a railway coal yard and a Victorian church called St Andrew's Presbyterian and, although the station remains, the coal yard and church are now gone.

Gravel Walk

Gravel Walk ran from Rose Lane into St George's Lane, finally sloping up to join St George's Terrace on top of the ramparts. It was very narrow and there was an ancient flint wall near the Rose Lane end, which was once the Augustinian Whitefriars' perimeter wall. Today, due to the Whitefriars retail development, most of Gravel Walk has been swallowed up by Fenwick's, formerly the site of Riceman's. The remainder retains the name, serving as an access road to Fenwick's fourth ground floor entrance. The following applies to an area no longer accessible as an historical street as it has now been swallowed up by the Whitefriars shopping development.

During the night of the June 1942 raid, Simon Langton Boys' School was badly hit. Children arriving at the school at the Gravel Walk entrance found just a few classrooms still standing. The remainder had vanished amid a pile of exercise books, papers, glass and lead. The boys wandered around in confusion but were naturally rather chuffed to be let off school. Some of them went to the post office in Stour Street to get jobs as volunteer messenger and telegram boys, and, for this important duty, they had to be sworn in and were allowed to wear special armbands.

In the 1930s, the Langton garage in Gravel Walk plied a busy trade and was run by a Mr G. Deakin and Mr R. Pollard. One of their charabancs was provided to take juniors from the Simon Langton Boys' School to their sports ground at Nackington, where the school eventually relocated in 1959. In 1960, the school buildings between Gravel Walk and St George's Street were demolished.

The Sun building was destroyed in the bombing of 1 June 1942, forcing the Sun Insurance company to take temporary, long-term refuge at No. 1 Castle Street. The new Sun building was completed in 1957 and remained for forty-two years until it was demolished to make way for the Whitefriars Scheme.

Among the businesses to survive war damage was E.J. Philpott Ltd on the south side and, a little further on, Drew's Coaches, just before the St Mary Bredin church burial ground.

Number 6 was occupied by W.S. Williams & Sons, coach-builders, as a paint store. It caught fire on 1 April 1964 and the many cans of paint produced a dangerous conflagration for the firemen to deal with.

Riceman's department store, now taken over by Fenwick's, was built on the Simon Langton Boys' School site in 1961, set back from the original frontage to allow for road-widening. Eleven years later, the Midland Bank office was completed, also occupying the site of the school, which had been used as a surface car park for the intervening years. A building to the left of Midland Bank, with pyramid-shaped skylights, contained the entrance and stairs for the Whitefriars shopping development. This, too, has now gone.

After the Simon Langton Boys' School had relocated, the north side of Gravel Walk was cleared and, in 1963, this land was used to widen Gravel Walk, while St George's Lane was also improved in this scheme. The Philpott's site, still standing at this time, went in 1965 and was replaced by a car park.

Halfway along Gravel Walk was the aforementioned old burial ground for St Mary Bredin church. The burial ground had probably been in existence since the 1870s although the church was demolished in 1942. In 1966, the gravestones were removed and, in 1969, the multi-storey car park was erected on the site, while the extension of Gravel Walk continued through to Watling Street. The people of Canterbury hated this ugly multi-storey car park and it was removed in 2001 as part of the Whitefriars scheme, which has now taken over the entire area.

Guildhall Street

Guildhall Street dates from 1806 and is named after the medieval guildhall at the junction with the High Street. The original guildhall was built in the late fourteenth or early fifteenth century and was known as the Church of the Holy Cross. It was demolished in the mid-twentieth century; the information available varies in respect of the actual dates.

A disgraceful exhibition of bad behaviour happened at Guildhall Street in 1832. The Archbishop of Canterbury, William Howley, had been invited to dinner with the Corporation members but the people were furious with the archbishop, who had refused to be enthroned at Canterbury a few years earlier, preferring to remain at his other two homes, Lambeth Palace and his country residence, Addington Park, near Croydon. He had the ceremony conducted by proxy, an action which deprived his subjects of a fine party and provoked angry letters to the *Gazette*. Bent on revenge for their disappointment, a mob gathered outside the guildhall and pelted the Archbishop with stones and lumps of mud, shouting abuse, causing the frightened gentleman to leap from his carriage and rush inside the guildhall. This was recorded as the archbishop's first visit – maybe also his last.

The fate of the medieval guildhall attracted a great deal of controversy but it was demolished in 1950 on the grounds that it was unsafe, sometime after it had infected its neighbour, Currys, with death-watch beetle. It was felt at the time that it would be too expensive to renovate. It had a Regency frontage, to the High Street, added in 1835 but a rather inferior Edwardian style to Guildhall Street. Architect Hugh Wilson presented a report to the city council in July 1948, detailing the problems, which included dry rot in the rafters, and, although all issues were carefully considered, it was agreed that it had to come down. The mayor at the time was Mrs Evelyn M. Hews, who remained in office from November 1946 to May 1949. The guildhall was duly demolished in 1950 and the site is now occupied by Clarks Shoes, who moved in during 1956 and underwent refurbishment in 1993.

At No. 7, Frederick Charles Snell started a business selling picture frames and fancy goods in around 1893 and, a few years later, the business took over No. 8, adding more toys and knick-knacks. Photographs taken at the time show a window crammed full of stock from top to bottom. (Later, during the 1930s, Mr Snell traded from No. 46 St Peter's Street.) Around this time, No. 9 was Nye's oyster rooms and No. 10 was the Ben Jonson Inn but, after the First World War, the buildings were occupied by William Lefevre Ltd and eventually became Debenhams.

Number 1 became the premises of Jay's Furnishing Stores after their shop at Nos 57-58 St George's Street was destroyed in the Blitz, although they returned to St George's Street in the 1950s. Next door to the Congregational church at No. 2, from the early twentieth century, was Burniston & Co. coal and coke merchants, whose property was taken over by P. Hawksfield in the 1940s.

The Congregational church was built in 1876 to replace an older chapel but it was closed and condemned as being unsafe in 1948. Subsequently, the building was bought by William Lefevre of Debenhams and became part of their store. The church was designed by John Green Hall, who was responsible for other churches in Canterbury, including the Masonic temple in St Peter's Place.

H

Havelock Street

Havelock Street is named after General Havelock, who distinguished himself during the Indian Mutiny and whose statue is in Trafalgar Square in London. Havelock Street is situated close to Military and Artillery Streets. It is nearer to the town than the other two streets and its Victorian terraces, which date from the 1850s, tend to be somewhat larger. There is a surprise halfway down these Victorian terraces: No. 19 is a public house, the New Inn, with its sign hanging over the small doorway. The New Inn, whose proprietors are K. H. and M. A. Temel, is licensed to sell alcohol either to be drunk on the premises, or to be taken away.

Continuing down Havelock Street towards Broad Street, on the right is the little day nursery, which boasts Joanna Lumley OBE as its patron.

The roof of the Eastbridge Hospital, 2004.

High Street

The High Street runs from King's Bridge to the Mercery Lane junction; after this it becomes The Parade and then St George's Street. This area comprised Canterbury's central shopping area even before the Second World War.

Close to King's Bridge, No. 25 High Street is the famous Eastbridge Hospital of St Thomas the Martyr, which was originally a refuge for pilgrims. The hospital has the distinction of being one of the oldest buildings in Canterbury. Its stone crypt dates from the twelfth century, while a fresco on the refectory wall is said to be 800 years old. The roof of the chapel on the top floor was constructed in 1287 by shipbuilders because they were the only tradesmen with the skills to create a design that could accommodate the large bell. The bell has been rung three times in recent history: first when Terry Waite was freed in Beirut on 18 November 1991, having been held captive for 1760 days; secondly, for the millennium celebrations; and, finally, when the Queen Mother died peacefully in her sleep on 30 March 2002.

The hospital has also been used as a library, a school and, in the sixteenth century, as an almshouse. At present, it houses eight elderly people in warden-assisted retirement flats and its chapels are still used as places of worship. The undercroft, with its transitional Gothic-style arches of the twelfth century, was the pilgrims' sleeping area and, during the period when the hospital was used as an almshouse, it was a coal cellar. In 1933, the undercroft was restored to its present usage and art exhibitions are held there. For example, during May 2004, Canterbury artist Susan Shaw was exhibiting her artwork *Shopping*, comprising rows of purple carrier bags standing side by side between the ancient arches, a challenge to consumerism.

At one time, a proposition was made to dismantle the front of Eastbridge Hospital and set it further back, to ease congestion and facilitate road-widening. Fortunately, this suggestion was never taken up.

Queen Elizabeth's Guest Chamber, 2004.

Opposite the Eastbridge Hospital stands King's Mill, granted by King Stephen to St Augustine's Abbey in 1144. Just over a decade ago, there was a doctor's surgery on the premises but now it operates as the Ask restaurant. Further along, on the same side as Eastbridge Hospital, is Queen Elizabeth's Guest Chamber, which was an inn for pilgrims. It is here that Elizabeth I met her admirer, the Duc d'Alecon, in 1573.

A terrible fire occurred at No. 6 on 18 August 1865, at the premises of an upholsterer, John Pout, allegedly by the tipping over of a pitch pot. It broke out in the evening and, although firemen fought hard to control the blaze, it did considerable damage to Nos 3-9. Those affected by this tragedy were the *South Eastern Telegraph* office at No. 3; a glass and china dealer, Jacob Abrahams, at No. 4; a confectioner, Mr Colcock, at No. 5; a shop selling music and pianos, proprietor George Eastes, at No. 7; and chemist, Sidney Harvey, at No. 8. The *Kent Herald*'s offices at No. 9 were quickly demolished to stop the fire from spreading to Guildhall Street. To a lesser extent, Grafton House, situated at the corner of the High Street and Mercery Lane and owned by George Wood the draper, was also damaged. It has been claimed that the fire started in a dormitory which was once part of the medieval Chequer of Hope Inn, which is now the premises of H. Samuel, the jeweller's (although they are planning to move to larger premises at the time of writing). On the opposite corner, Boots the chemist's building has two famous gargoyles lurking beneath the roof.

In the 1890s, Walter Cozens, a local historian who traded as a builder, occupied No. 37. This industrious philanthropist was a distinguished-looking gentleman with a white pointed beard and moustache and a black bowler hat, whose well-known book, published in 1906, was entitled *Old Canterbury*. Responsible for founding the Archaeological Society as well as the Canterbury Art Society, he died in 1928 aged sixty-nine.

By the end of the 1920s, two-thirds of the shops in the area belonged to locals: for example, Madame Stuart, milliner, was at No. 36; Arthur Bozon, confectioner, at No. 37; and Aitchison & Co. Ltd, opticians, at No. 38. The piano showroom of H.J. Goulden occupied Nos 39-40, although it was later destroyed in the Blitz.

Before the First World War, the Capital and Counties Bank Ltd occupied the premises now used by Lloyds Bank. Opposite the old bank was a shop called Hilton's. The Savoy restaurant, which was large enough to accommodate 160 people, was situated at No. 9 and run by Francis Pololi until the beginning of the First World War, serving lunch for 1s and afternoon tea for 5d. At this stage, it was taken over by Mr James Long, a keen businessman with another restaurant in Church Street St Paul's at that time, who continued until the 1940s. A few years later, the Savoy became a shoe shop called Blindell's.

During the 1930s, Gaywood's restaurant at No. 41 was Canterbury's solution for weddings, parties and celebrations and its large dining area and long rows of tables and chairs could comfortably seat 200. Its interior was decorated in Regency-striped wallpaper and there was a huge gilt-framed mirror between the two tall windows. The Sidney Woodman school of dancing used one of the upstairs rooms for some time after the Second World War and, around 1955, the room was used by dance teacher Hugh Connolly. (The Sidney Woodman school of dancing also had a spell in the late 1940s in Foresters Hall at No. 47 and presently operates in All Saints Lane.)

At No. 12, in the late 1940s, Currys were trading in a fifteenth-century timber-framed property, although alterations were made at later dates, leaving it with a mixture of fifteenth-, seventeenth- and nineteenth-century features. As it was next door to the rather decaying guildhall, Currys was infected with the death-watch beetle, although an attempt had been made by the guildhall to cover it up with lots of plaster! Eventually, Currys had to shore up their wall from inside the shop and from 1949 onwards the guildhall was gradually demolished.

During the 1940s, at No. 8, J.H. Dewhurst Ltd, butchers, operated in the same premises as the London & Scottish Assurance Corporation Ltd, and the Kleeneze Brush Co. However, a much earlier medieval building was hidden behind its nineteenth-century façade. Number 8 had a colourful history since, having survived a great fire in 1865 with just a badly burned roof, it survived a further fire in 1992, but needed some restoration. At No. 10, the Home and Colonial grocer's store traded, while No. 13 was the Maypole Dairy Co. and No. 14 was Lipton's Ltd. Mrs D.E. Callender was the publican of the Bell Hotel at No. 15, which originally sold George Beer and Rigden's ales but later changed to Fremlin's, finally closing down in 1974. Number 16 housed Clement Clarke Ltd, opticians.

The bombing of the south-eastern end of the High Street destroyed much of the area including St George's and St Mary Bredin's churches, the Longmarket, the Corn Exchange and much of Whitefriars.

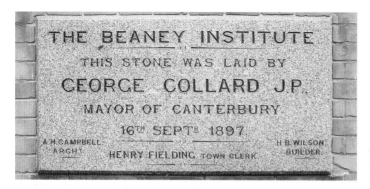

A sign outside the Beaney Institute dedicated to the mayor, 2004.

Old signs to the A2, 2004.

The Fleur-de-Lis Hotel dated from the fourteenth century, as indicated by its ancient timber-framed inner structure, which was hidden by an eighteenth-century façade. Its great age and historical value did not save the Fleur-de-Lis from demolition in March 1958, despite a hard fight from conservationists.

The George and Dragon Inn in the High Street was demolished in 1898 and the site was used to build the Royal Museum and public library. Known as the Beaney Institute, it was opened by the mayor, George Collard JP, on 26 September 1867. The Beaney Institute was named for its founder and financier, Diamond Jimmy, aka James Beaney, a labourer's son who was helped by local philanthropists. As a result, Jimmy went to Edinburgh to study medicine and served in the army and the navy as a surgeon. He then started up in business as a chemist, but unfortunately this venture was unsuccessful. So, opportunist James Beaney joined the gold rush to Australia in 1857 and, by the late nineteenth century was doing well, earning a great deal of money and writing medical papers, a success story which earned him his nickname. When he died, he left £10,000 for an institution 'for the education of the labouring man'.

A frequent visitor to the High Street during the 1950s was Dee Davie, who adored beautiful shoes. When she started work at fifteen, her father bought her a smart suit and opened a post office account for her, with £50, intended to set her up for adult life. Dee had never had so much money in her life and, in delight, set off for Canterbury shopping centre. In the High Street shoe shop (she thinks it was Bata), she was unable to resist the expensive pair of bright red pumps and spent all her doting father's contribution to her future on this one pair of shoes. She got into trouble, but never regretted the red shoes.

Above left: Dee Davie in her red shoes, 1959.
Above right: Goulden's piano shop at Nos 39-40 High Street. *(Courtesy of Doris Conroy)*

During the 1950s, wire pulley systems in shops were considered very modern. The famous Lefevre department store, which is now Debenhams, had a wool shop opposite, which sold materials and sewing machines. There were two young Lefevre sisters who served in the shop, using the old-fashioned wire pulley system. The salesgirl would place the money in a small casket and pull a handle. The casket would whizz along wires to the cashier at her station, who would then take the customer's money, replace it with the change and receipt, and send it back to the salesgirl to hand to the customer.

At No. 33, Baldwin & Son, household drapers, millinery and fashion goods, traded in a similar fashion with a wire pulley system, from their fine modern building next to the County Hotel. However, the building was not modern at all, for behind the façade were two medieval timber-framed buildings, standing side by side, as could be seen from the rear elevations, one having a gable end, the other a hipped roof and staircase turret. Baldwin's also had grand windows to showcase their wares but, sadly, the building was demolished in 1969 to make way for an extension to the County Hotel, which is right in the middle of the High Street. The car park at the rear is on the site where travellers once tethered their horses.

Unfortunately, of the nine grocer's shops that once plied their trade in the High Street, none now remain.

Above: Approaching the High Street from St Peter's Street. In around 2000 Hubble & Freeman closed and Cello now occupy the site, selling china and glass. Jumper is still there today. *(Copyright Stephen Bax)*

Hospital Lane

Hospital Lane runs from Castle Street to Stour Street and takes it name from the Maynard and Cotton Hospital, founded in the reign of Henry II for poor people. Originally, the meaning of the word 'hospital' was not limited almost exclusively to medical care; it simply meant somewhere those in need could find food and shelter. Rosemary Lane, which runs parallel to Hospital Lane, defines the boundary of the hospital gardens.

I

Iron Bar Lane

Iron Bar Lane, one of the small lanes that run between the main street and Burgate Street, was badly affected by the Blitz: some people say it was the worst affected of all the city's thoroughfares. Its topography changed from a variety of buildings, running down both sides of the street, to wasteland, although some garage buildings left over from the 1930s remained standing. Court Bros ran their business in Iron Bar Lane, until the Blitz left only the outer shell of the large building, which was once a depository belonging to Godden & Son, still standing. Also destroyed were Austen printworks, while all that remained of the Crown Inn, which stood on the corner of Iron Bar Lane and Burgate Street, was the chimney stack.

At No. 19 were the tailors Wilson & Waller but, after the Blitz, all that was visible of their former premises was the cellar with its rounded arch. During excavations behind Wilson and Waller's site, a medieval well and building foundations dating from the Roman period were discovered by archaeologists.

After the Blitz, some of the waste ground was used as a car park and, in spring 1952, Iron Bar Lane was widened and a car park built in the middle. At this time, Link Lane was constructed to run from the car park to Canterbury Lane. In the 1950s, shops were erected on the widened section of the lane, including a row of basic single-storey units on its east side.

Ivy Lane

Ivy Lane was once called Lodderelane, which means beggars' lane. During the early twentieth century, the lane contained a row of picturesque Tudor-style cottages formed from Wealdon

Picturesque Iron Bar Lane before the Second World War. *(Copyright Canterbury Library, local studies collection, Kent County Council.)*

House, a fourteenth-century building. During the 1960s, Wealdon House was renovated and made into a single dwelling called The Hall.

The blindmaker's in Ivy Lane, A.H. Amey & Sons Ltd, occupied premises, purchased in 1924, which were originally an oast house. Their main items of equipment were enormous sewing machines for fashioning the great quantities of blinds they produced. During the 1942 raid, the roof of their building was lost, although they stoically continued to trade from their lower floors. Later in that year, a new asbestos roof restored the building to its original state. From around 1970, Amey's operated under the threat of compulsory purchase as the city council wanted to extend the Longport coach park. The firm closed down in 1975, after a period of unease, and the building was subsequently demolished.

The three-star Chaucer Hotel which operates from No. 63, formerly a private Georgian house, says it has always attracted religious pilgrims.

J

Jewry Lane

Jewry Lane is situated behind the County Hotel in the medieval Jewish area. A synagogue stood nearby in Stour Street and there were around twenty families on the site of what is now the County Hotel.

K

King Street

King Street runs from Best Lane, parallel with Palace Street. Doris Conroy (*née* Rennell) has clear memories of her childhood there before the war, at No. 37 in a terrace called Highbury Cottages. 'Everyone in our street knew everyone else,' she says, 'and everyone was so friendly'. There were two older Rennell sisters, Gladys and Phyllis. Tragedy struck the family when a little boy was born who did not survive, so when Doris was fourteen in 1928, the family took in a baby boy just two weeks old. His mother was married but not to the baby's father and, although her husband thought he could accept the child, he later found he couldn't. The Rennells took in baby Peter in July 1928, but Doris' father died the following December and the girls also lost their mother at the end of the war, when Peter was sixteen. Peter now lives in Devon and although he and Doris are in contact by telephone, neither is well enough to travel the long distance to see the other.

When they were old enough, Gladys and Doris went into service, while Phyllis found work in a shop. Eventually, Doris married an army man and they had a son, Rodney, of whom she is justifiably proud. He became a Chief Petty Officer in the Royal Navy and served on the *Ark Royal* as a member of the aircrew. Once he was on *This is Your Life* with the film star and comedienne Hattie Jacques, who 'adopted' the helicopter aircrew and invited them to London to be on the show. 'He knew he wanted to be in the navy since he was about ten,' says Doris. 'He used to walk about swaying. He wanted to improve his balance for when he was at sea.' However, being in the Royal Navy wasn't all that Rodney Conroy expected. Once, when there was a review for the Queen at Portsmouth, everyone wore their very best uniforms,in spite of the fact that their ship was anchored several miles away. For the past ten years, Doris' son, sixty-five at the time of writing, has lived in Union Street, which runs between Military Road and Northgate.

Opposite Doris, next to the little graveyard of St Alphege's, was the lodging house of Mr and Mrs Bradford. Before they moved into No. 37, Doris' mother was worried the lodging house would generate too much noise, but in fact it was quiet. Auntie Molly Downer, the late sister of Doris' mother, remembered when monks lived in the lodging house. She was ninety when she died and was bewildered by the monks' habits, telling her niece, 'They're funny men, Doris. They wear frocks!'

There was an old synagogue on the north side of King Street, set back from the road, which is now a music room for the King's School. When Richard I was on the throne, the Jewish

Below left: Ninety-year-old Doris Conroy, 2004.
Below right: Rodney Conroy, Chief Petty Officer in the Royal Navy. *(Courtesy of Doris Conroy)*

people helped fund the Crusades, but, by the time of Edward III, the Jews had been expelled from England. It has been recorded that thirteen houses were left vacant. Many dignitaries rubbed their hands in relief, as their debts disappeared when the Jewish community left. However, when they returned, everything went back to the way it was and the courts were again busy with problems of debt. The Jewish cemetery can be found in the grounds of St Dunstan's. The cemetery, which has recently been renovated due to a grant from Lottery funds, contains 150 graves, dating from 1760 to 1930.

Several fine buildings were sacrificed to progress on the west side of King Street during the 1960s, including the Amos and Dawton auction rooms at No. 43, formerly the Eight Bells public house. Harold Dawton, who died in 1986 aged ninety-eight, was sheriff in 1946, mayor in 1953 and in 1954 and joined Frank Amos to form the auction rooms. The Prince of Wales public house at No. 51, at the other end of the row of buildings, was also sacrificed and, by 1962, the entire terrace had gone and was deeply regretted by many people in Canterbury.

L

Lady Woottons Green

Lady Woottons Green was originally Mulberry Tree Green but the name was changed in the seventeenth century to honour the wife of the owner of St Augustine's Abbey.

At No. 1 stood a Georgian house built on the ruins of the St Augustine's Almonry Chapel. The house was occupied in the 1940s by Miss Wiltshier, Miss Kemp and Mr Usher and was the only house in the street that remained undamaged by the June 1942 bombing. People complained that some of the other houses were not beyond repair and need not have been

Right: Signpost and gardens in Lady Woottons Green, 2004.

Opposite above: The house where Dickens wrote *David Copperfield*, 1910. *(Copyright Canterbury Library Local Studies Collection, Kent County Council)*

demolished but, apart from the one undamaged property, they were gone by 1943. The cleared areas were replaced by modern housing in 1955.

On the northern corner of Lady Woottons Green and Broad Street stood The Priory, although this, too, succumbed to the destruction. Between Lady Woottons Green and Broad Street was a post-medieval house associated with Charles Dickens but this was pulled down after bomb damage in 1942 and all that was left of it by the late 1940s was the cellar. The site was developed by building a neo-Georgian Diocesan House, which was opened by Archbishop Geoffrey Fisher in 1955. It was the first new building construction since the end of the war and boasts the date of its origins over the door.

Although much has changed about Lady Woottons Green, the green from which it takes its name is still there today. With its bright, formal flower gardens and benches on which to rest, it provides a colourful contrast to the traffic thundering along the ring road.

Lansdowne Road

This was where they used to keep the animals, ready to be transported by rail. Locals at the time complained of the terrible smell on hot days.

Lime Kiln Road

The name indicates that chalk was burnt here to make lime to be used in mortar for building work. This continued until fairly recently. Frank Cooper Ltd owned the limeworks and quarry at the end of the road, which is now an unmade single track road. Early in the 1960s, the works closed and, in the 1960s, the buildings were demolished – with difficulty, as the heat had hardened the brickwork.

Linden Grove

This little road was once Water Lane, as can be seen from signs on the wall. Another road is now assigned the name Water Lane.

Linden Grove was once Water Lane and both signs still exist on this corner wall, 2004.

Small Victorian terraces in Linden Grove, facing The Bishop's Finger (built in 1698), 2004.

The early twentieth century in Littlebourne Road. *(Copyright Canterbury Library Local Studies Collection, Kent County Council)*

Entering the city in Littlebourne Road, 2004.

Littlebourne Road

After the final, terrible bombing of 7 June 1942, a Sturry fireman was killed in the early hours of the morning when his engine fell into a crater.

In 1952, when St George's church was pulled down, carved stonework from the window jambs was carted here to make a nice garden wall for one of the more opportunist residents!

London Road

The Red House was occupied by the vicar of St Dunstan's from 1911 to 1920, although today it is a nursing home. Most of the properties in London Road are large, detached Victorian houses, many of which have become guest houses, hotels or nursing homes.

A few prefabs could also be found in a small estate leading off from London Road. Eventually, as traffic congestion increased, a diversion road, the A2, was constructed, cutting through fields and countryside, and named Rheims Way.

The London Road roundabout was originally built as a crossroads, but this proved a danger both to traffic and pedestrians.

The Longmarket

Turning off the right side of St George Street was The Longmarket, which fronted The Parade in the early nineteenth century and provided an indoor market which stretched to Burgate. The Corn and Hop Exchange was housed upstairs. In the early twentieth century, goods were set out on the ground but, by the 1930s, stalls had been erected selling bedding plants, flowers, fruit and vegetables, meat, confectionery and second-hand furniture. A woman called Rosie Coia, who always dressed in black, sold coloured ice-cream from a barrow in 1927. (She had also worked with her ice cream barrow, in Northgate during 1922.)

There was little in The Longmarket that survived the bombing of 1942 and the Regency Corn Exchange, as well as The Longmarket building, were taken down to first-floor level in June of that year. Locals remember that a gaping hole was left for some time at the edge of The Parade. During the autumn, it was suggested that the affected traders could operate from temporary shop premises inside the established Longmarket structure, but it took five years for this to materialise.

In 1946, the King, in full naval uniform, visited Canterbury with the Queen and Princess Elizabeth, and viewed the Norman remains discovered on the blitzed Longmarket site. They were welcomed with the customary bunting and a riot of Union Jacks hanging from windows. People did everything they could to catch sight of the royal proceedings, including

This page and opposite: War damage and rebuilding in The Longmarket in the 1940s and 1960s.
(Copyright Canterbury Library Local Studies Collection, Kent County Council)

climbing onto blitz-damaged pillars and balancing, somewhat precariously, on railings. One little boy was to be seen clinging grimly onto a bus stop.

Finally, as a result of the devastation, prefabricated shops were erected in 1947 and these were known as Ministry Huts. During the period of construction, the east side of Butchery Lane could be viewed through their concrete supports. These shops included a favourite of small children at that time, Hambrook's the stamp shop and, for the adults, a wine merchant, J.H.G. Hamilton. The surviving pre-war buildings, together with the prefabricated shops, were demolished in 1959 and a new shopping area in the minimalist style was begun two years later. It was unpopular with the people of Canterbury, who complained the shops were like shoeboxes, and pandered more to the needs of tourists than those of the people. Among the shops trading in The Longmarket in the 1960s was a radio and television shop called Murdoch's, taking up a prime position on the corner.

In 1990, The Longmarket development was demolished. A new shopping area was built but it caused even more controversy than the modernist buildings it replaced. Canterbury opinion was strongly divided but most did not favour the changes.

On a more optimistic note, an archaeological excavation during the 1990 redevelopment uncovered some valuable articles of Roman pottery, human remains, late Anglo-Saxon haircombs and medieval jugs in a cesspit. In addition, many of the changes that had occurred through the years had left their mark and, as a result, we now know that Terric the goldsmith once occupied one of the shops.

Longport

Longport was the site of a medieval market originally developed by St Augustine's Abbey, next door. St Augustine's, one of the oldest abbeys in England, was founded in 598, although it suffered some damage when Henry VIII ran amok dissolving the monasteries in 1538.

John Smith's almshouses, constructed with fine Dutch gables, date from 1657 and were intended as a place of refuge for poor people.

Peggy Poole (*née* Thornton) rescued several elderly ladies from Longport during the 1942 raids. She lived on the old Roman road Stone Street, on a farm, which was occupied by her parents from 1921-45. Peggy and her mother, Barbara, saw the city burning, so they went to investigate next morning and took the elderly ladies to the safety of Chartham. 'One was desperate to contact her bank,' recalls Peggy, 'and insisted I went to find it – down streets that were full of unsafe masonry'. So Peggy set off in the direction of Rose Lane, only to find the bank had gone. She tells how frightened she was when she was stopped by the police.

The former Kent and Canterbury Hospital complex, which dated from the late eighteenth century, was a familiar site at Longport. Peggy Poole remembers how Dr Douglas Reid took her eldest sister, Penelope, with him at Christmas to tour the wards and carve the turkey, for this was a time when family doctors really knew their patients and Dr Reid was aware that Penelope longed to be a nurse. Tragically, Dr Reid was killed in a plane crash in fog. Peggy says, 'He was beloved in the city. At his funeral, taken by the famous dean and broadcaster, Dick Sheppard, 3000 people packed the cathedral and many more crowded the entire length of the route taken by the coffin through the city's streets'. Sadly, Dr Reid's widow, Mary, was hounded by a reporter and when she refused to be interviewed, he invented his own story. Since Dr Reid's passenger, a lady not related to him, was also killed, the ruthless reporter had plenty of scope. Dr Reid's practice was taken over by Dr Lucas, his brother-in-law. Penelope fulfilled her ambition to become a nurse during the war and later married and became Lady Goodwin.

The demolition of the Kent and Canterbury Hospital had been planned since the 1930s. For a time, it was used as a boys' technical college because a new hospital had been constructed in south Canterbury in 1937. When a new technical college, which later became the Geoffrey Chaucer School, was erected in Spring Lane in 1967, the building was once again surplus to requirements. This fine building, having given good service both as a hospital and a school, fell to the demolition squad in 1972.

Building works in Longport revealed some Roman remains, including a fine floor which inspired an amusing comment by an intrigued American tourist: 'I wonder why the Romans built their floors underground.'

Lower Bridge Street

Lower Bridge Street was home to an early cinema and theatre, the Palais, which later became St George's Theatre. Its architects were Jennings and Gray and it had a circular vestibule, an auditorium with pink plaster walls and red chairs and, on the first floor, a tea room and a circle containing 200 seats. The opening film was *A Patriot of France or The Ordeal*, which played on 8 February 1915. One of the most memorable showings was *Ben Hur* in January 1928. On 22 December that year, *Phantom in the House* was shown, accompanied by RCA sound. The Old Stagers and the Canterbury Operatic Society also appeared there. The Co-op later purchased the building for their grocery store and allowed a dance hall to operate on the second floor, but this was closed due to the war. The building was demolished in April 1961. Situated on the corner between St George's Gate and Lower Bridge Street at St George's Crossroads, it had to make way for a roundabout, a necessary change as part of the second stage of the ring road, and subsequently the store moved to St George's Street. Another sacrifice to the new roundabout was tobacconist, confectioner and stationer, Pettit & Son, whose shop next door to the Co-op came down just before work on the roundabout began, in 1969.

The motor company, Invicta, owned many of the properties in the street, which experienced varying degrees of damage during the Blitz. Shops at Nos 6-10 were destroyed, although at No. 6, Tice & Co. heating engineers, speedily erected a single-storey building to replace their blitzed premises. The Dashwood Toy Shop was reduced to rubble and about nine people who lived in flats above the shops died in the raid, but most buildings from both sides of the street remained unscathed.

During the 1940s, the Star Brewery Stores, which sold George Beer and Rigden, was at No. 1a, and there was a doctor's surgery at No. 1, while the fishmonger, Mac Fisheries Ltd was at No. 2, although they moved back to St George's Street early in 1950, close to the site of their original, blitzed, shop premises. Number 3 housed the hairdressing salon, Lorna Hairdressers, providing curly perms to the locals, as was the fashion at this time, while No. 4 contained a confectioner and a restaurant, Dyson's, fortunate in being spared damage from the Blitz. The greengrocer, Dumbrell's, was not so lucky and traded at No. 5 in the ground floor, all that remained of a three-storey, late Georgian building.

At No. 14 lived hairdresser Herbert Santer. His shop was damaged in the Blitz but, because the shops on either side were undamaged, it escaped demolition for the time being and was not pulled down until 1950. The florist next door at No. 14a, owned by Mr P.E. Jackson, remained until 1969. According to the sign above his canopy, Mr Jackson sold 'Ryder's seeds, bedding plants, Dutch bulbs and shrubs', and the shop window had a fine display of plants and cut flowers. Mr Jackson and his wife were closely involved in local community projects and were the proud winners of the second prize in the 1953 Canterbury Carnival contest for the best-decorated vehicle. The Jacksons' Ford estate was topped, appropriately, by a crown of beautiful flowers and Mrs Jackson looked rather flowery herself in a crisp, floral summer dress, black gloves, black neckband and a flower corsage at her collar. Their little shop was finally demolished to make way for the second stage of the ring road.

The Co-op building mentioned above was demolished in April, 1961. Situated on the corner between St George's Gate and Lower Bridge Street at St George's Crossroads, it had to make way for a roundabout, a necessary change as part of the second stage of the ring road – and subsequently the store moved to St George's Street. Another sacrifice to the new roundabout was tobacconist, confectioner and stationer, Pettit & Son, whose shop next door to the Co-op came down just before work on the roundabout began, in 1969. The Saracen's Head, a seventeenth-century pub on the corner of Lower Bridge Street and Burgate, came down in 1969. (It is dealt with in more detail in the section on Burgate.)

During the early 1960s, the Brickies' butchers was next to the Invicta Motor Co. and was demolished in 1974 for an extension to Invicta's premises. Further down on the east side were the new headquarters of the Royal Insurance Group, opened by Lord Cornwallis, Lord Lieutenant of Kent and chairman of the London board of Royal Insurance. (Their previous premises were at No. 29 High Street.) The grounds used as a car park immediately in front of the building were once occupied by the Co-op but this site was also eventually used for stage two of the ring road.

The extended premises which had served the Invicta Motor Co. was demolished and a new purpose-built garage and showroom were erected during 1963. Invicta Motor Co. moved to a site in Sturry Road in the 1990s and shops replaced the Lower Bridge Street garage and showroom.

M

Martyrs' Field Road

This name commemorates those who died for their religious beliefs in the mid-sixteenth century. Forty-one Protestants – ten women and thirty-one men – were burnt at the stake for their opposition to the Catholic Queen Mary between 1555 and 1558. In 1899, after a public appeal by high-ranking locals, a memorial was erected in their name on Martyrs' Field. The list of names carved into the stone includes 'Bradbridge's widow' and 'Wilson's wife'. It is a sad irony that the proper names of these brave women have been forgotten.

Orchards once covered the ground where the Martyrs' Field estate now stands.

The dedication on the Martyrs' Field Monument reads: 'For themselves they earned the martyr's crown by their heroic fidelity they help to secure for succeeding generations the priceless blessing of religious freedom.

Mercery Lane

Mercery Lane leads from the main street to the Buttermarket and the cathedral gate and relates to mercers, who were sellers of clothes and textiles which were woven locally. A twelfth-century salesman, Solomon the Mercer, lived on the corner, selling, among other materials, silks and damasks. At the cathedral end of Mercery Lane stands Debenhams, which occupies the site of the medieval Crown Inn. The Debenhams restaurant at the north-eastern corner of the building is aptly named The Crypt as it was once part of a complex of medieval cellars that ran from the High Street along Mercery Lane and as far as Christ Church Gate.

A shop on the western corner of Mercery Lane and the High Street still has the stone arches that once belonged to the Chequer of Hope Inn. Cellars in the southern part of Mercery Lane belonged to the inn, which was built in the 1390s for pilgrims visiting Canterbury and was owned by the cathedral.

The proprietor of a dispensing chemist's at No. 11 in the early 1890s was Edwin Bigglestone, whose father, William Bigglestone, ran an iron and brass foundry with J.G. Drury in 1835. Mr Bigglestone's chemist's shop continued in business until the First World War.

In the early twentieth century, J.G. Charlton, photographer, opened his studio in Mercery Lane after moving from premises at No. 54 St George's Street. Mr Charlton eventually became the cathedral's official photographer and continued to run his business until after the Second World War.

In the 1940s, the premises of Lefevre & Hunt with its fine plate-glass windows bearing the ornate lettering of their business name were situated on the left, if facing towards the

Left: Mercery Lane street sign, 2004.

Opposite above: The Miller's Arms, 2004.

Buttermarket. On the opposite side, the tobacconist and confectioner E.A. Hart traded at No. 15.

Fortunately, during the June 1942 Baedeker raid, the flames caused by the incendiary bombs were prevented from reaching this quaint street of timber-framed houses through a change in wind direction. (see also Butchery Lane). There were only around fifty yards to spare, which must have been a great relief to the people of Canterbury.

Military Road

Military Road runs across the former St Gregory's Priory and was used as an approach to the nearby barracks, where, a large area of housing was erected for the army in the nineteenth century. The barracks were a popular meeting place for the East Kent Foxhounds hunt, who could be seen making their way along Military Road past the old Garrison church, now All Saints. Dressed in their finery, the huntsmen would enjoy breakfast in the officers' mess and then set off to Trenley Woods. In 1909, the master of the East Kent Foxhounds was Mr Selby Lowndes. Next to the barracks' official place of worship, All Saints' church, were riding stables but these have now been replaced by the huge Royal Mail sorting office. In 1954 the Sidney Woodman school of dancing presented the pantomime *Mother Goose* at the Garrison Theatre.

The Leopard's Head is one of Canterbury's newer public houses and was opened in 1959 on the site of a public house destroyed in the bombing.

In December 1961, demolition was in progress and the early nineteenth-century terraces on the east side of the road were cleared so the area could provide additional grounds for St Thomas' School. An ambulance station, costing a total of £36,500, was also included in the plans and was opened by the mayor, Ernest Kingsman, in February 1965. The ambulance service was first operational in 1945 and the original two ambulances were merely converted vans. In the new depot, there were seven modern ambulances and twenty-five staff.

Mill Lane

Mill Lane was once a much longer road, continuing along what is now Blackfriars Street, but it was diverted in 1247 when a stone wall was built around the Dominican Priory. The abbot of St Augustine's owned a mill, St Radigund's Mill, on the site opposite the Millers Arms public house at the junction with Pound Lane. The mill was destroyed by fire and now there is a building resembling a white tower on the edge of the site; this architect-designed house dates from the 1970s. While flour mills were the most abundant, there were also river-powered mills for fuel and parchment.

Monastery Street

Two famous gates are situated in Monastery Street, the fourteenth-century great Fyndon Gate dating from 1301, with its magnificent stone carvings; and the smaller Cemetery Gate of St Augustine's Abbey. Fyndon Gate takes its name from Abbot Thomas Fyndon, who built the abbey and royal palace. The monastery, whose ruins are approached from Longport, was founded after St Augustine's arrival in Canterbury and rebuilt after the Norman Conquest but, of course, Henry VIII dissolved it in 1538. Charles I and his wife, Henrietta Maria, are said to have spent their wedding night here.

Monastery Street has many variations in architecture, including a house, dating from around 1790, whose upper part is mathematically tiled . Mathematical tiling made a house look as though it was built of red brick. The tiles are thin but they overlap and are pointed to look authentic.

Left: A good example of mathematical tiling in Monastery Street, 2004. *(Copyright Stephen Bax)*

Above and left: The annual regimental reunion of the Buffs, on parade Sunday 1 August 2004.

N

New Dover Road

In the 1940s, at No. 2, on the corner of Chantry Lane, lived the Andrews family – mother, father, two sons and a daughter. Their home served both as a private dwelling and the father's accountancy business. Mr Andrews had thoroughly reinforced the basement of this large house with strong wooden supports and the family left camp beds down there in case of an emergency. On the night of the 1942 raid, they had retired to the safety of their basement when someone knocked on their door to report a fire. 'It appeared one of those incendiary breadbaskets opened right above us,' said Leslie Andrews. The family had to get out via the front door and race across the road to Maltby's fire station for safety, from where they watched their home and business being consumed by the flames.

In Barton Fields, originally No. 21, stood a fine Victorian house, Pinecroft, where the solicitor Cecil Kingsford lived for many years. In 1920, Pinecroft became St Helen's School for Girls and its headmistress was Miss Winifred German. In the 1930s, the building reverted to private ownership.

St Christopher's School, established in 1925, was run by Miss Clements and Miss Arrowsmith. Peggy Poole says, 'Miss Clements lived to a great age and there was a celebration in the city when she reached ninety.' Peggy and her siblings started their education there 'along with the Roses, who were the four sons of the Bishop of Dover, and June and April Twyman, who lived opposite the school'.

Eventually the area was redeveloped so that, by the 1960s, on the corner of Lower Chantry Lane and New Dover Road, stood the new showrooms, workshop and stores of Caffyn's Ltd. Caffyn's, who sold commercial vehicles, already had premises on the opposite side of New

On 6 October 2004, shortly after writing this account, fifty firefighters were called out to deal with a fierce blaze at the Courts branch in New Dover Road. The damage was severe.

Dover Road but they wanted to expand because they were in competition with the Itnvicta Motor Co. and Barretts Motors. At No. 7 stood the British Legion House, which was also demolished in the late 1950s, to be replaced by showrooms and offices for Caffyn's.

In February 1967 the post-war prefabs were dismantled. The prefabs had proper concrete roadways and each was named after a theme: for example, war leaders, giving rise to Churchill Road, Montgomery Avenue, Mountbatten Avenue and so forth.

The old fire station later became Courts Mammoth Stores. On 6 October 2004 this Court's store was severely damaged by fire (see photo on previous page). Court's went into liquidation in December 2004.

Northgate

Close to the junction with Union Street, Mr Sinclair, chimney sweep of R. Sinclair & Sons occupied premises at No. 101 in the early twentieth century. He was one of nine or ten sweeps in Canterbury at this time. Sweeps' equipment was simple, just a collection of rods and a brush that were easy to operate. One length of rod would be slotted into the stiff, round brush, which

The original toilets in St John's Hospital, Northgate. The effluent was directed by channels to be washed away by the River Stour. Men and women used the same room but different benches. *(Copyright Stephen Bax)*

would then be pushed up the chimney to its full length. Another rod would be slotted into the first, and another, till the brush burst through the chimney into the sky. Children enjoyed watching from outside a house whose chimney was being swept and their shouts of glee told the world the brush had exited the chimney pot. Housewives had a busy time of it afterwards, for there was always a residue of soot which fell down the chimney and coated the rooms below. Wise housewives covered the furniture with old sheets and curtains before the sweep arrived.

Also in the twentieth century, George Thompson ran his photographic studio at No. 70. Up until the 1930s, Joseph O'Brien milked his six cows in a stable and shed situated close to the turning into New Ruttington Lane.

The Canterbury Cine Club used the old Prince of Wales Institute in the 1930s for rehearsing and filming. Actresses were more modest in those days as, in 1934, the *Kent Herald* had to spread the word that the club was in need of more ladies for their productions.

Just off Northgate is a cul-de-sac, St John's Place, and there was a school here that started before the First World War, the old City Council school for girls, boys and infants. The school was proud of the trophies won by its children at the Kent Music Festival in the 1930s.

At No. 60, the Paveley family has run its bookbinding business for the past eighteen years. The family has been involved in bookbinding as far back as they remember and Len Paveley is proud to claim that the Paveleys were originally French Huguenots. Originally, they were called the Pavely family but, in the 1876 census, an extra 'e' was added accidentally, and they became Paveleys. Little has changed over the years and son Christopher runs the business in much the same way as his father, grandfather and great-grandfathers. They have bound family bibles, university theses, coroners' reports for the county courts and various tomes for royalty, including the late Queen Mother and the late Princess Margaret. Naturally, due to the sensitive nature of much of their work, they are bound by the Official Secrets Act. Prior to the Paveleys occupying No. 60, the premises were a pine furniture shop and, before that, a greengrocer's.

Next door to the Paveleys, at No. 60a, Julie Johnson runs the Canterbury Doll's House Shop. Julie, who was born at Canterbury Hospital forty-five years ago, lived in a prefab in Downs Road until she was three and since then has always lived around the Canterbury area. At the time of writing, she had been forced to hang a 'Closing Down Sale' sign in the window due to falling sales, which are probably due to the establishment of a doll's house fair at Westgate Hall. In 1999, Julie operated at No. 45 Palace Street. She moved on to No. 39 Northgate a year later in order to take advantage of cheaper rent but it didn't seem to help! Previously, No. 60a was a tanning shop (suntan machines, not leather) but it is now located a few doors down at No. 53. Nearby is the boutique, Bon Marché, which used to be the Hobby Shop, selling doll's house kits, needlework kits, semi-precious jewellery and beads. Julie Johnson remembers it with nostalgia as being an Aladdin's cave but, unfortunately, it vanished around ten years ago.

A few years ago, a pair of old cottages was demolished to make way for the new premises of Bishop's Taxis. On the opposite side of the road is the Institute of Heraldic and Geneological Studies, deemed to be Britain's longest-established resource for researching family history.

Prior to the widening of Union Street in 1960, Northgate was the main road into Canterbury from Sturry. The Two Brothers public house at No. 91 was lost to the redevelopment in the mid-1960s. Numbers 55-57, next to the Model Tavern at No. 54, were demolished in the late 1950s and a car park was built on the site for the patrons of the public house until it closed down in the 1980s.

The last building on the left of Northgate, on leaving the city centre, is the Northgate Medical Centre and this used to be a car park. Further round to the left, the huge Sainsbury's building can be seen, incorporating unusual architectural features. Long white round pillars extend from its roof, which caused Canterbury residents to comment, when it was being built around seven years ago, that the plans were upside down. I am told the architecture works in the same way as a suspension bridge.

North Holmes Road

Saint Martin's church in North Holmes Road dates from around AD 597, and has the distinction of being the oldest church in England in continuing use, even incorporating some brickwork from Roman times. Apparently, Queen Bertha worshipped at St Martin's church during the seventh century and used nearby Queningate, or Queen's gate, to approach it. Queningate is now a car park. Queen Bertha is said to have met St Augustine there in AD 597. The Christ Church College also stands here, an Anglican foundation for teacher training, built in the precincts of the former St Augustine's Abbey, whose chapel has a strikingly modernist aluminium and glass roof.

North Lane

North Lane looked very different during the early twentieth century, with attractive, ancient cottages that were lost in the war due to enemy action. During 1909, there were severe floods when a three-day period suffered four inches of rain, forcing tradesmen to drive their horses and carts through waterlogged streets.

Detail of reused Roman bricks on the south wall of St Martin's Church, North Holmes Road. (Copyright Stephen Bax)

The Great Stour runs between houses of North Lane and Pound Lane, 2004.

North Lane suffered greatly during the Blitz and only two fine properties survived the post-Blitz demolition. No. 57 was finally dismantled in 1951 and is now occupied by the North Lane car park.

More old houses on the east side of North Lane were destroyed in February 1956, to accommodate road-widening and also improve the car park. The buildings opposite, however, are still intact today.

W.E. Pinnock and P. Hawksfield & Son were merchants who distributed coal delivered by rail to the West Station Coal Yard in North Lane. The coal yard became redundant in the 1980s and now accommodates a housing estate.

Next door to two picturesque old cottages at Nos 39-40, is a single-storey building which stands in front of the old coal yard, and this is No. 38, The Flower Studio. A former fishing tackle shop, it has been run by Kenny Stanton for the past six years. Before the fishing tackle business, it was a bike shop selling mopeds, but the right to trade was withdrawn by the council because the owners persistently repaired the vehicles on the street. Kenny believes that during the 1960s, the shop was connected to the old coal yard. The wall on the left of the building once belonged to another building, now long gone, and the single-storey building that now houses The Flower Studio was, apparently, tacked on to this wall. An interesting detail about the premises in the 1960s is that a pit was constructed in the centre of the floor,

The Flower Studio in North Lane, 2004.

housing a machine with huge ball bearings. This was used to grind down various substances for the chemical industry. The items were reduced so thoroughly that they were finer than talcum powder and they were then delivered to ICI and Pfizers. 'The whole operation would be illegal nowadays,' Kenny points out. Around this time, there were also riding stables at the back of the property.

While the first and second stages of the ring road went ahead, the third stage did not, which saved a terrace of cottages – Nos 46-49 – from demolition. By the mid-1970s, however, they were empty and mostly boarded-up. Fortunately, shortly after this, a new city council was set up, which formed a conservation department aiming to preserve the city's heritage. They swiftly cancelled the third stage of the ring road to avoid further demolition.

Nunnery Fields

Nunnery Fields originally belonged to the Benedictine Priory of St Sepulchre on the corner of Oaten Hill and the Old Dover Road but the priory was closed in 1837. Its most famous nun, Elizabeth Barton, was executed in 1533 for predicting the death of Henry VIII when he divorced Catherine of Aragon. She is remembered today as the Holy Maid of Kent.

Census results give an insight into how Nunnery Fields has changed. In 1841, there were only Nunnery Cottages. It was an agricultural area: the census listed six agricultural labourers, three labourers, one bricklayer, one milkman and one cellarman. There were two females: one of independent means, the other a dressmaker. Twenty years later, the 1861 census shows twenty houses, the most impressive change being that now eight houses had female heads of the household, their main occupations being domestic trades such as dressmaker or laundress. The men's occupations, however, had expanded. Not only were there the usual labourers but also a grocer, painter, shoemaker, millwright, drayman, railwayman and engineer's apprentice.

In 1891, just thirty years later, partly due to the expansion of the railway, there were fifty-two houses, some of which had their own servants. There were now twelve female heads of household, all domestic, and the male heads of household included brewer's labourers and the chief warden of H.M. Prisons.

According to Pike's Local Directory of 1897-1898, No. 1 was a post office and at No. 7 there was a butcher's owned by Cedric Hills, with an abattoir situated behind the shop. William Coppen, at No. 18, was a builder and a beer retailer, while a public house at No. 25 was run by a baker called Edwin Coppen. It was called Two Doves and still remains today.

Marjorie Young, who lived in Nunnery Fields at the time of the raid of 31 May 1942 recalls that it was the most beautiful evening, with 'a clear blue sky,as though it was cut out of cardboard.' Another lady who lived in Nunnery Fields during the raid remembers emerging from her house the day after the bombing and putting out chairs and a card table for homeless people, then serving them tea provided in buckets by soldiers. She remembers how distressed many of them were because their teeth had been put to soak for the night and they were unable to rescue them. Some wore coats over their nightclothes, some had only their nightwear and others pushed prams or barrows with a few belongings grabbed from smouldering ruins. Eventually, the lucky ones managed to find shelter with relatives but others had to remain out in the open or in farm buildings.

O

Oaten Hill

Oaten Hill was once the site for a cereal market for Canterbury, as the name suggests, but prior to that, the city gallows were here. In front of the Old City public house is an ancient burial mound, now flattened to accommodate a car park and to the left of the public house is an oast house. In the 1950s, the Cross Keys public house incorporated Kingsfield Bakery in its premises, but in the 1960s the bakers was replaced by Martin's Electrical, although this has now reverted back to the Cross Keys public house.

Old Dover Road

During medieval times, traffic entered Canterbury along Old Dover Road and down Oaten Hill and Dover Street. The original Roman route was down Old Dover Road and the street currently named Watling Street. New Dover Road opened in the late nineteenth century then, in 1981, the A2 bypass diverted traffic away from the city.

A carpenter, joiner and undertaker called Frank Muir lived at No. 77 before the First World War. Many businessmen practised more than one trade in order to survive and often these trades were diverse. Frank Muir's, however, seemed a sensible combination of trades; no doubt he fashioned the coffins to supply his undertaking business. Number 77 was a fine house with shutters and window boxes and looked more like a public house than an undertaker's business.

J.C. Pine ran his greengrocer's in one of a row of three-storey buildings, which were originally built in the early 1890s. They were later replaced by cottages which attracted the unfortunate name, Rats' Row. There was also an old fire station for the city but it was a makeshift affair, occupying what was formerly St Lawrence Farmhouse, together with some corrugated iron sheds which were added on in 1943.

In the 1940s, No. 7 was the Riding Gate public house, run by publican Alfred Banham. It was damaged in a small raid in 1942. It may have been swallowed up by the fire station, whose main frontage is on Upper Bridge Street.

Further along, an inn called The Sign of Dover, situated next door to Ye Olde Forge, was a receiving office for buses and cabs. It was also distinctive for having a public telephone. The inn was closed during the First World War and, in 1927, it was renamed Sundial House and became a private residence.

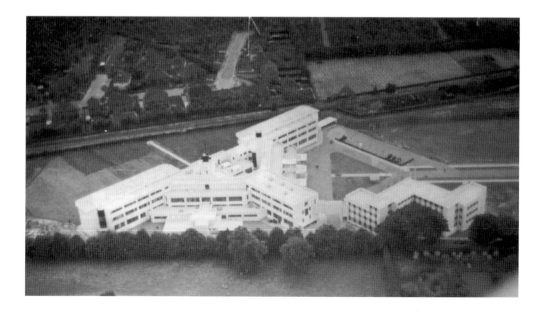

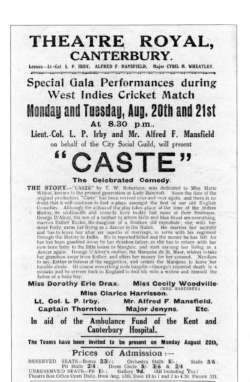

THEATRE ROYAL,
CANTERBURY.
Lessees—Lt.-Col. L. P. IRBY, ALFRED F. MANSFIELD, Major CYRIL M. WHEATLEY.

Special Gala Performances during
West Indies Cricket Match

Monday and Tuesday, Aug. 20th and 21st

At 8.30 p.m.,

Lieut.-Col. L. P. Irby and Mr. Alfred F. Mansfield
on behalf of the City Social Guild, will present

"CASTE"

The Celebrated Comedy.

THE STORY.—"CASTE" by T. W. Robertson, was dedicated to Miss Marie Wilton, known to the present generation as Lady Bancroft. Since the date of the original production, "Caste" has been revived over and over again, and there is no doubt that it will continue to find a place amongst the first of our old English Comedies. Although the action of the play takes place at the time of the Indian Mutiny, its sentiments and comedy have to-day lost none of their freshness. George D'Alroy, the son of a mother to whom birth and blue blood are everything, marries Esther Eccles, the daughter of a drunken old reprobate; she, with her sister Polly, earns her living as a dancer in the Ballet. He marries her secretly and has to leave her after six months of marriage, to serve with his regiment through the Mutiny in India. He is reported killed and the money he has left for her has been gambled away by her drunken father, so she has to return with her new born baby to the little house in Stangate, and start earning her living as a dancer again. George D'Alroy's mother, the Marquise de St. Maur, wishes to take her grandson away from Esther, and offers her money for her consent. Needless to say, Esther is furious at the suggestion, and orders the Marquise to leave her humble abode. Of course everything ends happily—George's reported death is a mistake and he arrives back in England to find his wife a widow and himself the father of a baby boy.

| Miss Dorothy Erie Drax. | Miss Cecily Woodville |
| (MRS. HARDISTY.) |

Miss Clarice Harrison.

| Lt. Col. L. P. Irby. | Mr. Alfred F. Mansfield, |
| Captain Thornton. | Major Jenyns. | Etc. |

In aid of the Ambulance Fund of the Kent and
Canterbury Hospital.

The Teams have been invited to be present on Monday August 20th,

Prices of Admission :—

RESERVED SEATS—Boxes **23/-** ; Orchestra Stalls **5/-** ; Stalls **3/6** ;
Pit Stalls **2/4** ; Dress Circle **5/- 3/6 & 2/4**
UNRESERVED SEATS—Pit **1/-** ; Gallery **9d.** (All Including Tax.)
Theatre Box Office Open Daily, from Aug. 13th, from 10 to 1 and 2 to 4.30. PHONE 321.

J. A. JENNINGS LTD., "City" Printing Works, Canterbury.

Opposite below: The new Kent and Canterbury Hospital in Old Dover Road. *(Courtesy of Peggy Poole)*

Left: Gala Performance for the Kent and Canterbury Hospital. *(Courtesy of Peggy Poole)*

The first major development in Canterbury after the Second World War was the Simon Langton Girls' School, constructed on the site of existing playing fields. The school was designed in the art–deco style by architect Hugh Wilson, who began work in 1948, and was completed by 1951.

At No. 67, at the junction with Cossington Road, stood The Bridge House Tavern, which burned down in 1962. It was rebuilt and appropriately renamed the Phoenix. Keith and Linda Barker were originally customers and then became landlords. They took over the licence in February 2000 and are still there today. Business is good and, as Linda says, 'The pub sells itself.'

The flint wall is all that survives of the Hospital of St Lawrence for leprous monks, founded in 1137. When leprosy began to die out in England, the hospital closed down, along with its controlling partner, St Augustine's Abbey. Its name survives thanks to the nearby cricket ground and several small roads, closes and courts prefixed St Lawrence.

Old Ruttington Lane

The roots of the Saxon name Old Ruttington Lane are 1000 years old. The spelling has varied over years, in 605 it was Drutinstraete, in 1165 Drutintune, in 1200 Druthinton. It means 'street of the royal personage' because Queen Bertha passed along it to worship at St Martin's Church. It is one of the oldest thoroughfares in the country and also one of the oldest street names in existence. It extends around the northern and eastern precincts of St George's Priory. During the twentieth century, people lived their entire lives in this little lane, which seems to have been self-sufficient. At the bottom of the lane, there was a general store, where you could buy almost anything. Biggs, the bakers, produced bread that smelled heavenly and there were two butchers: a pork butcher called Mr Post at one end and Mr Boorman at the other. The local women did not need to go into town if they chose not to.

Old Ruttington Lane was developed during the late nineteenth and early twentieth centuries, with terraced houses to serve the families of soldiers at the barracks. The lane became a target for slum clearance in the early 1960s. At this time, at No. 15, lived Miss Cook, Mr Thomas Lewis occupied No. 16 and next door at No. 17 lived his neighbour, Mr Abdul Karim. After the demolition of these houses, the site was used for the St Thomas' Roman Catholic School. By October 1961, the row of houses which included Nos 38-42 was also empty, ready for the huge clearance.

Orange Street

This is the only street in Canterbury named after a monarch: William of Orange, who became William III. At the junction of Orange Street and Palace Street, there is a red pump fastened to the wall of No. 1, which was used to keep rushes damp at the nearby rush markets. Number 1 was occupied during the mid- to late nineteenth century by Mummery Brothers, tanners and leggings manufacturers. At this time, Orange Street was called Prince of Orange Street. Once, this stretch of road from Orange Street as far as St Alphege Lane, was simply called Red Pump. Today, at No. 1 stands the Seven Stars, a lively public house, keen on karaoke.

Dover's artist, William Burgess, was born in Orange Street in 1805, where his parents' coach-building business was located. William Burgess was a boyhood friend of the 'cattle artist' T.S. Cooper who lived in St Peter's Street. Cooper began to learn coach-painting prior to becoming a nature artist and it seems likely his original choice of career may have been due to his friendship with William Burgess.

At No. 8, on the corner of Orange Street and King Street was the Glutenia Foods Co., who made diabetic products and whose premises had a façade which hid a medieval timber structure of much greater antiquity. Glutenia may have been a victim of proposed road-widening in the late 1940s; certainly it was gone by 1950.

Orange Street also suffered some damage during the Second World War. One woman had her baby under a table during the bombing and wanted to be taken to relatives in Thanington. The task of transporting mother and child fell to ambulance driver Ruth Taylor of Cossington Road. When the men went into the house with the stretcher, the young mother simply walked out the door, carrying her newborn child. She climbed into the ambulance without any fuss and Ruth Taylor drove her to Thanington through all the rubble and devastation.

The gable end of the Freeman, Hardy & Willis shoe repair depot.

There was once a theatre in Orange Street. During wartime, dances were held on the premises. It now operates as a delightful emporium known as The Merchant Chandler, which boasts that it's 'The Most Interesting Shop' in Canterbury.

Orchard Street

As its name suggests, although it is hard to believe today, there were once fruit orchards this close to the city centre. Orchard Street is an attractive street with some interesting architecture, including old Victorian and Edwardian rows of cottages. Approaching from the High Street, on the right a short way into the street at No. 18 is the frontage of the old repair depot of the shoe shop chain Freeman, Hardy & Willis, although only the gable end shows their name immediately above the windows. Freeman, Hardy & Willis went into liquidation in the early 1990s.

Two well-known public houses have graced Orchard Street: the old Black Horse, first registered in 1837, and, on the corner with Cross Street, the Builder's Arms, although the latter has now been demolished. The Black Horse was originally part of the Canterbury brewery chain George Rigden & Co. and there is a stone placed by the company in a dividing wall in the building, engraved with the date 1909.

BURLINGTON

REGISTERED BRAND OF
DISTINCTIVE FOOTWEAR
SOLD ONLY BY
FREEMAN,
HARDY & WILLIS
LTD
━━ at their 470 Branches ━━

**LADIES'
BURLINGTON.**

Shoes

Glace Kid, 10/11

Box & Willow
Calf ... 11/6

Boots
14/9

**GENT'S
BURLINGTON.**

Shoes
14/9

Boots

Glace Kid, 16/11
Box Calf, 18/6

This choice brand stands in the very forefront
of popularity, and is a true guarantee of excellence
and high value.

It embraces a wide variety of smart styles, so
constructed as to ensure absolute comfort, while
their perfect fitting and shape-retaining qualities are
a source of pleasure to the most critical wearer.

To places where we have no branch,
goods will be sent by post on receipt
of order and remittance. Foreign
remittances must include cost of postage.

**Write to-day for Illustrated Booklet
Dept. P., Rutland Street, Leicester.**

P

Palace Street

Palace Street is one of the best-preserved streets in Canterbury. Its name is derived from the Archbishop's palace, which was replaced by Archbishop Lanfranc after a fire in 1067. The street was originally called Alphaba Street after St Alphaba's church.

A famous house in Palace Street is Sir John Boy's House. Sir John was an MP and recorder of Canterbury. The house was built around 1612 and leans over at an alarming angle to the northeast, the tilt apparently caused by a twisted chimney and falling bricks, which led to eventual collapse of the stack. This left a void in the centre of the building but now the house is supported internally by a steel cage. Twenty years ago, it was still the Old King's School Shop and the frontage bears the date 1647. No doubt Michael Powell, eminent film director and ex–King's pupil, was kitted out for his school uniform in the shop. The house is a fine example of pargeting, which, through incision, makes ordinary plaster appear like rusticated stone.

Above: A Palace Street sign.

Left: Sir John Boy's House is now an antique shop.

Opposite: A Freeman, Hardy & Willis advertisement.

A hermaphrodite woodcarving at No. 8 Palace Street, 2004. *(Copyright Stephen Bax)*

Opposite below: Detail from Conquest House.

Like today, there were a variety of trades and small shops plying their wares and services during the nineteenth century. In the mid- to late nineteenth century, there was Mummery Brothers, tanners and legging manufacturers, as well as butchers, chemists, boot- and shoemakers, tailors and cork-cutters. From 1882 to 1898, No. 6 was occupied by an Italian family, the Offrendis, who were confectioners and pastry cooks. In 1902, these premises became a restaurant run by Messrs Mazzuchi and Locatelli but, by the 1920s, they were occupied by a teashop owned by A. Tyrrell. Now No. 6 is a Children's Society charity shop.

Number 8 dates from the thirteenth century and is embellished with unusual woodcarvings. It was a priest's house, later enlarged to become a private dwelling. From 1882 to 1908, it was a tobacconist's and haircutting establishment.

The record of residents at No. 10 goes back to the thirteenth century. In 1862, Thomas Newman became the occupier. This was the year No. 10 became the Bell and Crown public house, named to commemorate the wedding of Princess Alice, second daughter of Queen Victoria, to Prince Louis, with the bell representing the church bells that rang to celebrate the royal occasion. In 1882, Henry Bailey became the innkeeper. At this time, Nathan Moses was a fruiterer at No. 11 but the Bell and Crown was later extended next door.

In 1882, No. 12 Palace Street was a boot warehouse belonging to Thomas Lavender. In the 1920s, it became a confectionery establishment run by Mrs M. Gardner. Today, it is a clothes shop.

In the early twentieth century, No. 13 belonged to a cork manufacturer, James Thomas Samson. Later, it was a fried fish shop, which continued trading for sixty years, and then became a restaurant. A butcher called George Wilkinson lived at No. 15 and the Albion Inn, whose licensee in 1882 was John Jackson, occupied No. 16. The Albion had a shady reputation and closed around 1908. In the 1920s, No. 16 opened as a hairdressers' salon run by the Greenstreets. The first Mr Greenstreet's son, Charles, took over from his father after the First World War, cutting hair and selling Brylcreem to the locals until the 1970s. Charles Greenstreet was most particular about his hair and would only allow one person to cut it, an assistant called Tommy Lennox. Now the premises are occupied by a gold- and silversmith.

Number 17, Conquest House, is a famous address, for this is where the four knights plotted to murder Thomas Becket. The stone cellars are said to date from the eleventh century, while the timber-framed gallery is from the thirteenth century. A most attractive building, it is ancient and crooked and well-suited to its current use as an antique shop. Number 18 was an outbuilding to Conquest House and horses negotiated the nearby passageway to get to the stables and yard behind the buildings.

In 1900, No. 19 was home to Miss Nethersole, a dressmaker. Forty years later, it was a tea room and No. 20 was a baker's and confectioner's, providing teas and light refreshments. Currently, it is an Indian restaurant. There is a single-storey structure between No. 20 and No. 21, which was used as a painter's store around a century ago. The proprietor was Robert Ratcliffe, who also had an address at No. 22, where, according to a street directory of 1882,

Unusual tiling at No. 21a Palace Street.

Detail of tiling at No. 21a.

he listed himself as plumber and gasfitter. This multiplicity of trades was not unusual at this time, probably due to unreliability of regular work. Number 20a is now a gallery, No. 21 is the RSPCA charity shop and No. 22 is a boutique for tall women, aptly named Dizzy Heights.

Around the 1890s, Walter Hunt's printing works and stationer's was at No. 41. It was later taken over by John Hunt, who sold toys, games, china and books. Eventually, the business became Hunt, Snell & Co. but the premises were destroyed in the Blitz. Next door to Walter Hunt, Nos 42-43 contained the printers, Gibbs & Sons.

At No. 55 in the 1920s, Clement Clarke, the optician, tested the eyes of Canterbury's citizens while W.A. Roper, a bootmaker, attended to the comfort of their feet. At No. 59 was the Mayflower Restaurant, where, in the seventeenth century, Robert Cushman negotiated the hiring of the *Mayflower* so the Pilgrim Fathers could set off for America. In 1882, George Mence Smith was the proprietor. Now, the teashop Butterfields operates from these premises.

Nos 60-61 date from the early nineteenth century. A Mr John Hobday lived here in 1878. He was a gentleman of many talents, describing himself as a cabinet-maker, upholsterer, auctioneer, appraiser, house agent, decorator and undertaker. Maybe the offering of several skills was necessary at this time in order to live reasonably well. Nos 60-61 are presently an Italian restaurant.

For thirty years, Tony Wright traded in stamps at No. 29 and Albert Anderson ran the cycle shop next door at No. 30. However, in the 1950s, Wright's took over the cycle shop premises and expanded the business to include cards, general stationery, jokes and novelties. In the 1960s, Wright's Stamp Shop also gobbled up No. 32, a fruiterer's originally belonging to a Mrs Jarrett, which meant three shop windows of Wright's Stamp Shop were divided, one pair from the single, by a domestic window. Mr Wright was helped by his wife Nina and mother-in-law Mrs Wells. Currently, the shop at Nos. 29-30 sells maps and guidebooks for tourists, while No. 32 is now the Book Palace.

Opening their store for the first time in 1927, Featherstones Ltd, 'Head to Foot Outfitters and General Providers to the Thrifty', occupied Nos 41-43. They took over No. 44 after the Second World War and then, in 1957, moved to Burgate Street, where they remained until 1970.

Number 48 was the King's School, built in the late eighteenth century. Classrooms were added for the junior school in 1914. Two famous novelists attended the school: Sir Hugh Walpole in 1896 and Somerset Maugham in 1885. The latter's fear at seeing the school's prison-like appearance on his arrival for the first time inspired a scene in his novel *Of Human Bondage*.

Number 50, opposite the Children's Society charity shop, was occupied during the nineteenth century by Mrs Escott, maker of stays and corsets, and No. 51 was the birthplace of Rupert Bear's creator, Mary Tourtel, on 28 January 1874. Today, Mary Tourtel's old home is an art gallery. Samuel Cordwell, an artist in glass, lived at No. 52 in 1882 and next door was occupied by Mr J.M. Watson, a travelling draper.

Pat and Bill Griffin went to live at No. 52b after their wedding in Canterbury Cathedral in 1976. They met when Bill gave Pat piano lessons. Bill first came to Kent to take up a teaching position in 1964 and continued for seven years. In 1967, he joined the choir of Canterbury Cathedral, singing bass, and stayed for twenty-one years. After their marriage, Pat taught first-year pupils at Beauherne (meaning 'beautiful heron') Primary School. Number 52b was an upper flat, flanked on both sides by self-contained houses, and the young couple's rent was cheap for the time. 'It was a knock-down price of £2 a week,' says Bill. This was a privilege granted by the cathedral, who owned the property. It suited the Griffins even though it was tiny: Pat remembers that the little wooden staircase was so narrow that on moving-in day, one man had to carry Bill's piano upstairs on his back. A few years later, when she went to hospital to have her baby, she had to walk downstairs as there was no room for a stretcher. The flat was unsuitable for a baby so Pat and Bill moved to a house in nearby Whitstable – a timely event since the cathedral put up the rent at that time.

The Griffins remember their Palace Street neighbours. A very old lady lived in the flat downstairs and she enjoyed the advantage of her own small courtyard. Next door – on

Two pretty bridesmaids in the cathedral grounds on the Griffins' wedding day in 1970. Bekky Esshack, aged seven, is on the left with sister Jainy, aged nine. *(Copyright Pat Griffin)*

J. Gray's butchers, Palace Street in 1987. *(Copyright M & M Collins)*

Crowds waiting outside J. Gray's during the Pope's visit in 1987. *(Copyright M & M Collins)*

J. Gray's is now a juice and smoothies bar.

Melanie and Malcolm Collins took over No. 58 Palace Street in 1979. Prior to 1978, it was a clothes shop. *(Copyright M and M Collins)*

the right if facing the buildings – lived another cathedral singer called Roy Locke. Part of his property was later sold to become a ladies' underwear shop. Next door to Mr Locke, a fishmonger plied his trade, while on the left of the Griffins, another self-contained house was occupied by a cathedral carpenter and his wife, Mr and Mrs Norman.

The Parade

The Parade is the continuation of the High Street, after it crosses Mercery Lane and St Margaret's Street. St Andrew's church, which was Georgian with a Victorian porch, once stood on the south side of the Parade but the redundant church was demolished in 1956 to accommodate an extension to the Westminster Bank next door.

At Nos 8-9, on the corner with St Margaret's Street, stood the premises of West & Son, drapers and milliners, whose business started prior to the 1880s and continued until the First World War. It is thought this medieval building was once a resting place for pilgrims.

The Parade once had a fine hotel, the Rose Hotel, but this building was gutted during the June 1942 raid. Fortunately, the Rose Hotel was the only casualty suffered in the Parade.

Pin Hill

The most famous landmark along Pin Hill is the Dane John, a tall mound whose name is a corruption of 'donjon', the Norman word for a castle keep. It was originally an ancient burial mound and the Norman motte and bailey castle would have dated from around 1070. During the eighteenth century, the mound was reshaped and Alderman James Simmonds had the monument built at the top. The shape of the monument is probably the reason for the name Pin Hill. Years ago, the Dane John was treated as a place for an outing and was controlled by a beadler, Mr Horne, who wore a navy uniform, a peaked hat and carried a silver walking stick, with which he terrorised the local children. Opposite the Dane John is the huge Bizz nightclub.

Above: The Dane John is in the background of this old photograph.
Below: This guest house, which was once the old courthouse, on Pin Hill was built using the original city wall.

Pickfords Removal and Storage had an enormous warehouse at the end of Pin Hill and Cheyney & Co., who made scales, occupied a large Victorian building on the corner. Neither company trades here today.

Pin Hill contained a mixture of Victorian and Edwardian houses, some of which were demolished to accommodate the ring road, including Nos 1-4 in 1969. Number 5 was the home of Frederick Richards but this fine detached house was also demolished for the sake of the ring road. The Man of Kent public house, which dated from the fifteenth century, and incorporated two seventeenth-century cottages and a nineteenth-century extension, all fronting Worthgate Place, served the local community. Like the Victorian and Edwardian houses, the Man of Kent was threatened by the plan for the ring road but in the end was unaffected and still exists today as the Round House.

Pin Hill became a dual carriageway in January 1970, during the second stage of the ring road construction. The road was extremely busy and dangerous to cross so a concrete footbridge was constructed in 1971. This footbridge provided a safe crossing for pedestrians from Canterbury East station to a footpath on the city wall ramparts.

Pound Lane

Until the Second World War, cattle and sheep were driven through the Canterbury streets to market. Stray animals ended up in the pound, located in aptly named Pound Lane, and could be recovered by their owners for a fee.

Pound Lane can be found immediately on the left after passing under the Westgate. On the corner of Pound Lane and St Dunstan's Street stands a music school which was once an early police station, erected in 1829. Very little has changed inside, so that today music students learn their skills in old police cells. The police station was rebuilt on the Riding Gate roundabout in February 1965.

Further along to the left is a stretch of the city wall originally built from Westgate to Northgate and financed by Archbishop Sudbury between 1380 and 1390. The Archbishop was murdered in 1381 during the Peasants' Revolt. Further on, the semi-circular tower at No. 16 is also part of this ancient city wall but a new frontage was added to the tower in 1870 when it became a private dwelling. It is now occupied by a firm of architects and surveyors.

The part of Pound Lane near the bend just before the Causeway was once an area much prone to flooding. One of the houses in this stretch of the road, No. 53, is called Farthing Cottage.

An old sign inscribed directly onto the bricks of the Music School in Pound Lane.

The Precincts

Ordinary people occupied many of the dwellings in the cathedral precincts. During the Second World War, barrage balloons tethered to the ground by metal cables helped defend the built-up areas from low-level raids. A fine barrage balloon was in evidence on 4 June 1942 in the Green Court, while its proud crew were inspected by the Duke of Kent.

Many people praised the dedication of the cathedral fire-watchers for the fact that the building escaped damage during the bombing. However, the Victorian library was destroyed and the deanery damaged, although it is now repaired and back in mint condition.

At No. 4 lived Lois Lang-Sims, together with her mother, cousin and her cousin's baby. The cousin's husband was in the army and stationed at Dover and, naturally, she wanted to be close to him. At about 12.45 a.m. on the night of the Baedeker raid of 1st June 1942, Lois Lang-Sims noticed that it was getting lighter, despite the rules of the blackout. She went to the window to look and saw that the Precincts were glowing in a pink light, due to great flares falling from above. She roused the others and all of them huddled together, trying to protect the baby between them, while planes roared, bombs screamed and glass smashed. Plaster even fell on their heads. By three o'clock, it was over and the gatekeeper's wife told them to vacate the building before it caught fire. Like many others, the family was struck by the sheer beauty of the flames reflecting on the cathedral. At the edge of the Precincts was a Georgian house belonging to Canon Macnutt. The house was a sheet of flame but luckily its occupant was away at the time.

A frequent visitor to the Precincts was Margaret Babbington, born in 1878, who was the daughter of the vicar of Tenterden. A staunch friend of the cathedral, she was regularly involved in fund-raising. She also managed to import eminent conductors and soloists for the cathedral, as well as working for the Kent County Nursing Association. During the war, she belonged to the WVS and was a familiar sight on her bicycle. She was once seen rescuing the bicycle from bomb rubble then jumping back on it and riding away. She often lectured, including in America, but in 1953 her health failed and she became a regular visitor to the Kent and County Hospital, mainly for her arthritis. She died in 1958.

During the 1950s, two senior teachers at the Simon Langton Girls' School, Miss Campling and Mrs Green resided in the Precincts with their maid, Beatrice.

It is not only ordinary people who inhabit the Precincts. One or two ghosts also hang around the area, the most famous of which – next to Thomas Becket, of course – is Nell Cook, who

Nell Cook, whose ghost haunts the Dark Entry.

disappeared after poisoning a friar and was found buried under a flagstone. It is said that Nell's ghost haunts the Dark Entry and anyone who sees her suffers death within a year.

Priory of St Jacob

This road contains the site of a hospital founded in the twelfth century for leprous women, although the old graveyard is closed and locked up today. In medieval times, people believed that to help the poor was to help Jesus Christ. Master Feramin, who founded the hospital, was claimed to be a Canterbury doctor and a member of Thomas Becket's household.

Q

Querns Road

All the families who lived side by side in a row of cottages in Querns Road were victims of the Blitz. The Bates family lived in one of the cottages. Three of the Bates children were in the Morrison shelter, while their mother and elder sister remained upstairs asleep. When the ceiling fell down, they too went to the shelter, while about sixteen houses around them burned. Two of their neighbours were killed and one of the children recalls her horror at seeing parts of pet rabbits blown to bits and hanging in the pear tree.

Next door to the Bates lived Mr and Mrs Woolgar with their children, Peter and Heather. As soon as the sirens sounded, Mr Woolgar herded his children down to safety but almost immediately they heard the aircraft diving and the next moment the door crashed in, injuring the mother and two of the children. Later, when their father returned to the house with a neighbour, both men were hit and killed but Mr Woolgar wasn't found until some time later because he'd been buried under the rubble. There is a sad and ironic footnote to the story: Peter remembered seeing his father's body with a smile on its face and recalled that Mr Woolgar was always called Smiler. On the other side of the Woolgars lived Mr Kemp, whose rabbits were also blown up by the bombing.

R

Rhodaus Town

Rhodaus is of Anglo-Saxon origin although we are not certain of its meaning. It may be because the cattle-market was held in Rhodaus Town on the city's eastern outskirts. The

Saxon for horned beast is 'rhither' and Rhodaus may be derived from this. St Mary Bredin School was built in 1860 on a Roman burial mound but was closed in 1940. During the war, it operated as a restaurant and by the mid-1950s the land had been purchased by Rootes Ltd, who owned a garage complex next to the site. Rootes made a great effort in the year of the Coronation, sprucing up their premises and mounting on their roof a royal shield with the letters ER, topped by a coronation crown. Today the site is the Canterbury Motor Company, a used-car dealership.

In the late nineteenth century, the Olympia skating rink, later called the Pavilion, was next to the school.

Roper Road

Roper Road was originally called Hanover Place, after Hanover Lodge at No. 50 but during the First World War people took offence at the German name and around eighty residents signed a petition to have it changed. The name Roper was taken from the house, now long gone, of the famous medieval family (*see* St Dunstan's Street). Hanover Lodge, which was occupied by Robert Stockdale in the early twentieth century, later became known as Holme Lodge and is now Chaucer House.

A photographer called Charles Allen lived at No.1 during the 1880s. The studio had closed by 1890. By this time, there were around six photographer's studios in the city and possibly the competition had become too fierce.

Number 20, a three-storey building with an attic and large bay windows on the first and second floors, housed the Canterbury Electric Welding Co. The business was started by John Vissenga in the early 1920s and continued until the late 1950s. John Vissenga was said to be a crack photographer who filmed local events in the 1930s.

Lenley's, the furniture showroom, occupies Nos 25-34. Before they moved here from the present Laura Ashley site in Burgate, during the 1980s, the Roper Road site functioned as a wood merchants. Lenley's was started by Leonard Watts and Stanley Adsett, the firm's title being derived from the first syllable of Leonard's name and the last syllable of Stanley's. They also owned a vegetarian restaurant in Love Lane called Stannard's, a name created in a similar way.

Rose Lane

In 1867, the St Mary Bredin church was built in Rose Lane but it was destroyed during the terrible air raid in 1942. After the bombing, the small chapel at Nunnery Fields was made available for worship until compensation from the War Damage Commission during the 1950s enabled the city council to approve the erection of the present parish council church. In 1956, Messrs Denne's tender for the work was agreed and Bishop Rose, from whom this lane takes its name, laid the foundation stone. The people of Canterbury helped to raise money to pay for the work needed, inspired by the slogan, 'Every £1 donated to build the new church buys a brick.'

During the summer of 1946, there was much excitement in Rose Lane as the Canterbury Excavation Committee dug out some open cellars to see if Roman buildings found in Butchery Lane and the Parade extended into the lane. The results were a little disappointing but there was evidence of a tiled Roman drain. In 1952, the cellars were filled in and Rose Lane was widened. Barretts of Canterbury Ltd built a new shop in the area in 1953, which was later taken over by C & H Fabrics. The former Rose Hotel site was also developed in the mid-1950s.

A garage, Marlowe Motors, was built on the space left by a casualty of the Blitz and was opened by Jack Warner. To the right of Marlowe Motors, an office block and showrooms were built in 1965 and named Watling House. Both buildings were pulled down to make way for the Whitefriars development.

Rosemary Lane

The lane is thought to have been named after the the aromatic herb although, with St Mildred's Tannery at the top, it couldn't have smelled too sweet here.

On the corner of Rosemary Lane and Church Lane St Mildred's stood the British Oak public house, a seventeenth-century building with a timber-framed roof. It closed in 1931 and remained boarded up until it was pulled down in 1948, although the ground floor walls remained until the 1950s, to provide an enclosure for a car park. Another interesting building, rendered in white, housed the English Fruit Co.

In 1962, terraced houses from the early nineteenth century were destroyed in a slum clearance scheme. The Cardinal's Cap public house was saved and still supplies locals with liquid refreshment.

S

St Alphege Lane

The church of St Alphege was built during the fourteenth or fifteenth centuries. In 1888, its interior glass and fittings were restored by Mr R. Carpenter. The church gave protection to the puritan Huguenot refugees who had been persecuted on the Continent for their beliefs. St Alphege's stopped functioning as a religious establishment in April 1982 and became the Canterbury Urban Studies Centre. It is now the Canterbury Environment Centre, founded in the early 1970s and moved to the converted medieval church in 1983. The venue is used for exhibitions, lectures, workshops and resources by members of the local community. The saint after whom the church is named was a true Canterbury stalwart, refusing to submit to the marauding Danish Vikings. He forbade the English to pay a ransom for his life so the Danes murdered him at Greenwich.

A variation of the spelling of St Alphege?

In the seventeenth century, Robert Cushman and Sarah Jekel were married at St Alphege church. Robert Cushman, who had negotiated the hire of the *Mayflower* for the Pilgrim Fathers was later excommunicated for failing to attend church and jailed at Westgate. Eventually, he too sailed off to the New World, no doubt feeling somewhat aggrieved at his treatment in the old one.

St Dunstan's Street

Most of the buildings in St Dunstan's Street appear today as they did many years ago. One of the most interesting landmarks is the Roper Gate, one of the best examples of Tudor brickwork in Canterbury. This gate, with its elegant arch and stepped gables, was the entrance to the Roper family home, Place House, and is all that is left of the original dwelling. This important monument fell into disrepair but was restored a few years ago by the conservation section of the city council.

The Ropers had a colourful history. An early member of this old family, John Roper, was Attorney-General for the notorious Henry VIII. John's son, William, married Margaret More, the daughter of Sir Thomas More, Henry VIII's Lord Chancellor, who was beheaded for his resistance to Henry's divorce from Catherine of Aragon. A loyal daughter, Margaret ensured that after her father's execution, his head was interred in the family vault at St Dunstan's church. John died in 1574 but the Roper family remained important among the Kent gentry.

In 1870, Roper House at No. 12 was built by Mr Frederick Flint of Flint & Sons for his personal residence. The large brick Victorian Gothic mansion was a means to display the Flints' personal wealth as well as their exalted position in Canterbury society.

Flint's brewery was situated behind Roper Gate and drays were seen pulling their carts through the gate to begin their rounds. The brewery was founded in 1787 and supplied many local public houses. In the late nineteenth century, there were around thirteen brewers in Canterbury. This was balanced by the number of public houses – around 165 – which has gradually reduced to the 50 now in existence. The site became a scrap metal yard a few years ago, although the oast houses are still in evidence. The cellars of the brewery still exist

The House of Agnes.

A detail of the House of Agnes.

beneath the industrial units, where a young girl was murdered during the 1960s, her body discovered by a local butcher.

For the Ropers of the early twentieth century, the house was expensive to maintain and so, in 1907, it became a private boarding school for girls and was run for some time by two elderly ladies, the Misses Jenner. Then it changed hands again and Dr Harold Wacher moved in. Around the 1930s, it was the Roper House Hotel and in the 1940s it became the home of the Royal School of Church Music. Today it is owned by the Royal National Institute for the Deaf, who provide support for thirty-four deaf and deaf-blind adults. A terrace of four renovated period cottages called West Place, inside the grounds of Roper House, is used as self-contained accommodation for residents who wish to be independent. The complex includes a craft workshop and a training room for teaching living skills and provides day care and outreach services for people living in the community.

At No. 15, W. Hopper the baker began in business in the late nineteenth century, after which the shop became Mrs Pugh's Sweet Shop. The front of the shop was converted by erecting a brick façade to hide the sixteenth-century timber-framing. No. 16, St Dunstan's House, is also timber framed. This fine house also dates from the sixteenth century and the façade was changed around 1750.

To the right, if facing in the direction of the Westgate, there is a building that looks as though it is toppling into the street: the sixteenth-century House of Agnes. The name refers to Agnes Wickfield, a character in Dickens' novel *David Copperfield*. Agnes was a real person, the daughter of the solicitor whose name is used in the novel. The first-floor bay windows were added in the seventeenth century and the ground-floor ones in the eighteenth century. Prior to the 1950s, the House of Agnes was a private house, occupied by Lt-Col. E.R. Bromhead, who leased it for twenty-one years from December 25 1916, with options to terminate at the end of seven and fourteen years. The rent was £70 per annum, which was probably good value because a sink with hot and cold water had been installed! In addition, it boasted a smoking room and boudoir on the first floor. The present owner, Mr John Durcan, has occupied the house for thirteen years. This fascinating inn and hotel provides an excellent showcase for his collection of curiosities, including a pair of fine forge bellows which serve as a low table in one of the bars. Also close to the Westgate Tower, but on the opposite side of the road, is the fourteenth-century Falstaff Corus Hotel, at Nos 8-10. The hotel provides additional accommodation in a restored wood mill. Both the House of Agnes and the Falstaff Hotel, which was then known as the White Hart, were probably used as accommodation for

The Falstaff Hotel, 2004.

travellers arriving in Canterbury after the curfew, as they were outside the city walls. The White Hart changed its name to the Falstaff in 1783, in honour of Shakespeare's colourful character. In the nineteenth century, it was a coaching inn, popular with travellers en route from London to Dover.

At No. 19 is the sixteenth-century public house, the Unicorn, which had a shady reputation as a bawdy house in the eighteenth century. The County Gaol stood conveniently next door! The medieval inn called the Bishop's Finger, which faces the Linden Grove turn-off, was originally the George and Dragon.

Number 47 was a butcher's around the beginning of the twentieth century but is now a bank, which has an example of mock glazing on the bricked opening on the Orchard Street side of the building.

St Dunstan's House, on the west side of the street close to St Dunstan's church, is a medieval building transformed by additions and alterations. The brickwork probably dates from the late eighteenth century. Some murals on the first floor, discovered beneath the wallpaper, were photographed by the Canterbury Archaeological Trust prior to conservation work.

In 1945, the butcher's shop in St Dunstan's was W & R Fletcher Ltd. There was also the County Laundry and an electrical contractor called Sidney Terry Ltd. Number 82 was the St Dunstan's Restaurant, owned by William Peters, who was also a confectioner and a baker. His business was The Model Bakery during the 1920s. A builder and undertaker, Mr Bateman, moved into No. 82 around 1930 and later the premises became a hairdressing salon.

At the junction of St Dunstan's Street and Westgate Grove was the St Dunstan's Café, distinctive with its mock-Tudor frontage. The property was turned into an antique shop called Ben Lee's but became a café again when the shop closed in 1980.

The St Dunstan's level crossing originally had manually operated gates but automatic gates were installed during the early 1970s.

The Westgate tower, which separates St Dunstan's Street from St Peter's Street, was utilised during the Second World War. A room in the tower was adapted to be an emergency control centre. There was an observation post and air-raid siren mounted on the roof, which was high enough to help people to spot enemy planes on their way. Nowadays, the Westgate Museum occupies this medieval, fortified gatehouse and visitors who climb to the top are rewarded by an amazing panoramic view of the city from its battlements.

St George's Gate (St George's roundabout)

The road called St George's Gate was created in 1801 from a short section of the main street, taking up the space left after the demolition of the gate itself. The road no longer exists, being buried somewhere beneath the St George's roundabout, which was constructed in 1969. From the 1890s until the Second World War, this was a pleasant trading area, where iron railings separated the street from the cattle market. The East Kent Club was situated further down towards St George's Street. Opposite the market, at No. 2, was the St George's Supply

Stores while next door, at No. 3, stood a tailor's shop, E. Williams & Son and James Craik had his photographic studio at No. 4, on the corner of Burgate Lane. From the beginning of the twentieth century until the early 1920s, No. 2 was occupied by Godfrey & Co., who sold pianos. The goods were delivered in a fine cart pulled by Taff the horse and the back of the cart advertised all their other branches: London, Brighton, Portsmouth, Ryde, Bournemouth, Weymouth, Exeter, Southampton, Aldershot, Gravesend and Chatham. These buildings were destroyed during the Second World War.

Number 1 was the only building to survive the Blitz. It was occupied by Pettit & Son, who were tobacconists. After the war, E.R. Bates' gun shop, with its timbered frontage and huge window, stood prominently on the corner. The building was erected to replace their original blitzed property. Mr Bates clearly liked to diversify as a variety of other goods, such as children's pushchairs, would be displayed outside the shop, beneath a signboard advertising, cycles, repairs and sports goods, as well as gun products.

St George's Lane

In the 1920s, St George's Lane was narrower than it is now. It had a forge and an oast house owned by Cooper and Wacher, hop merchants. It was always opened just before the hop-picking in August by the two elderly gentlemen who ran it. They lit the furnaces and dried the hops, which arrived by horse and cart. Sometimes, the old gentlemen allowed children to enter the premises and baked potatoes for them on the furnaces.

The City Printing Works were owned by J.A. Jennings Ltd, who printed the *Kent Herald* from the beginning of the twentieth century until the 1920s. The firm was originally at 8 Guildhall Street but moved to St George's Lane in the late nineteenth century. The works were destroyed in the 1942 raid. The firm took up temporary printing works at Harbledown Place, Summer Hill and set up a reception office in the High Street.

There was also a building company, Brownings, which was run in the early twentieth century by a man called Kennet. He was contracted to do work for the barracks at the time of the First World War.

Simon Langton Boys' School occupied the west side of the lane. It was built in 1914 and had a distinctive frontage with three gables. There was a gymnasium on the ground floor and classrooms on the first floor. The buildings were damaged in the 1942 raid and the school relocated to Nackington in 1959. The buildings were demolished in 1960 and the playground was used to widen the road. By 1962, construction was well underway on the large Riceman's department store on the former site of the school.

St George's Place

The old Regal Theatre opened at No. 43 with a capacity of 1,750 seats. The main feature film on opening day was *Falling for You*, preceded by a Walt Disney *Silly Symphony*, a *Magic*

Carpet story and *British Movietone News*. ABC took over the cinema from 29 April 1935. Entertainment was also provided next door in the ballroom, which ran the popular afternoon tea dances, while on the first floor was a café. A popular turn at the Regal ballroom was the Eddie Newport Dance Band. On 31 October 1942, after the matinée of *Gone with the Wind*, a Focke-Wulf bomber hit the rear of the cinema, destroying the ballroom and the café. The Regal closed in February 1943 and Eddie Newport and his band went on to perform at the Foresters Hall in the High Street.

In 1964, the Regal, now known as the ABC, was managed by Brian Pritchard, who did his best to attract people to the shows with modern kung fu films and the occasional publicity stunt. By 1972, the cinema needed an extra entrance as it was accommodating both filmgoers and bingo players. The ABC cinema with EMI bingo later converted to the Cannon cinema with Coral bingo, then Cannon reverted to EMI, and, finally, the building was refurbished under new management and became the Odeon in 2001.

Before the Second World War, there was a row of town houses occupied by professional people along the north side of St George's Place. They had three storeys as well as a basement and had louvred window shutters. The terrace, from No. 5 to the turning into Lower Chantry Lane, was bombed during the Blitz. A large section of the north side of the street became covered in trees and shrubs although, hidden amongst the vegetation, were the premises of building contractors, G.H. Denne & Son Ltd. The buildings that survived the Blitz were those near to St George's Crossroads, which included Seymour Browne, watchmaker at No. 3 and Clark, Hunt & Co. Ltd, who supplied the building trade, at No. 3a. Then there was a gap, presumably due to the bombing, and next door, at No. 4, was the Isle of Thanet building society. Finally, on the other side of some insurance companies, G. Twyman & Son Ltd had their premises on the corner with Lower Bridge Street. Fisk-Moore's photographic studio was at No. 7 but Mr W. Fisk-Moore moved to Burgate Street after his property was destroyed in the Blitz.

In March 1954, the new offices for the *Kentish Gazette* were opened on the north side of St George's Place. Like other buildings, they had been set back from the road to allow for the road to become a dual carriageway, which happened in 1969.

Nos 26-28 were Georgian houses and although they had survived the Blitz, they were demolished in 1971. After the houses were cleared, an office development, Rutland House, was erected.

Martin Walters Ltd, who sold cars, occupied a garage at No. 41, formerly the premises of Tapley Motors Ltd. However, the little garage was not large enough and the firm decided to build two prefabricated garage buildings on the gardens behind some bombed properties between the garage and the Baptist church. In the 1950s, the garage showroom was extended so that it stretched from the Baptist church (built in 1860) to the Regal cinema. At a later stage, a temporary building erected on the site of No. 41 also became a victim of the Blitz. Martin Walters Ltd continued to progress, redeveloping in stages, and St George's House, which had probably been built around the late eighteenth century, was demolished to accommodate their plans. The house had been a private home then, in the 1930s, a doctor's surgery and was subsequently occupied by the Pearl Assurance Company, auctioneer Arthur Mason and the Kent County Council planning department.

The south side of the street, having suffered less bomb damage than the north side, accommodated several financial companies in one of its Regency terraces, including the Liverpool & London & Globe Insurance Co. Ltd, the Temperance Permanent Building Society and Britannic Assurance Co. Ltd. In January 1949, the only house in this terrace that was a private dwelling was No. 28. Most of the properties were eventually demolished to make way for an office development.

Courts Furnishers, as mentioned under New Dover Road, also has a frontage on St George's Place, although the building is now severely damaged by fire and Courts went into liquidation in December, 2004. Formerly the site was occupied by the garage, Caffyns which was demolished in1984. Before the garage was built, there was a row of houses here, including the home of a GP and his wife, Dr. and Mrs Lucas.

The Safeway Supermarket appeared in the 1980s. The Odeon cinema still stands on the corner of St George's Place and Upper Bridge Street and next door is a row of trendy shops and restaurants.

Part of the Millennium Mural celebrating Canterbury's past and present, painted by Elisa Hudson. It adorns a subway running under the former market area of Canterbury.

St George's Street

Number 47a is where photographer Henry B. Collins started his business before moving on to St Peter's Street in 1894. Henry was once commissioned to take a photo of a boys' club which specialised in swinging Indian clubs, a popular sport of the period. Apparently, there was quite a technique to the art and a number of boys from Simon Langton Boys' School were involved.

In the early twentieth century, Arthur Francis Colbourne, photographer and artist, ran his studio at No. 58, having previously traded from No. 18 Castle Street. He proudly advertised the fact that he was 'Patronised by H R H Princess Beatrice and the late Prince Henry of Battenburg, His Grace the Archbishop of Canterbury, Le Compte de Barral, J. Henneker.' The fact that, in 1564, playwright Christopher Marlowe was allegedly born in premises previously occupying the site of the studio added to Mr Colbourne's mystique.

Another photographer residing in St George's Street was J.G. Charlton, although he moved to Mercery Lane around 1900. During the 1940s, Jay's Furnishing Stores occupied the site of Nos 57-58.

In 1911, at Nos 12-13, the Palais de Luxe cinema was opened by W.R. Sprague. Its claim to fame was that, in case of fire, everyone could be evacuated within thirty seconds. Mr H.G. Wilson took over the cinema in February 1913 and renamed it the Canterbury Cinematograph Theatre. The venture was unsuccessful due to the stiff competition and it closed down in 1915. David Greig the grocers moved in but the building was destroyed in the Blitz.

The Blitz destroyed the entire south side of St George's Street, from Whitefriars Passage to St George's Lane. The bombing damaged St George's church, in which Christopher Marlowe

Above: A detail of the clock in the St George's tower.
Right: The St George's clock tower.

was christened, as well as Marlowe's house. The clock on the church stopped at the moment of impact, twenty minutes past two. The main church had to be taken down immediately for safety reasons but the tower still stands, thanks to a canon of the cathedral who objected to its demolition in 1942. The tower and remaining ruins continued to cause controversy: the Holden Development Plan of 1945 planned to keep the tower as a permanent memorial to those lost in the Canterbury Blitz but the subsequent 1947 Wilson Plan pushed for its removal. Finally, it was agreed to preserve the tower, in view of its twelfth-century origins, but demolish the remainder of the church ruins. No one is sure what happened to the five church bells in the tower, although it is assumed they were destroyed in the raids. Restoration of the tower took place from 1953 to 1954 and a row of shops was built around it. They were pulled down in 1990 and new shops had replaced them by 1993. Other buildings in St George's Street were also severely damaged in the Blitz. For example, a wool business, Fleming, Reid & Co., was reduced to rubble in the bombing. The offices of the *Kentish Observer and Canterbury Chronicle* were also damaged and then the flames moved up the street, consuming one business after another. Among those burned were Gambrill's outfitters, the Lyon's cake shop, the Kraft shoe shop and the White Lion Hotel. The Canterbury Club at No. 33 which provided a place of relaxation for gentlemen with its fine snooker tables and armchairs, was destroyed. Parade Chambers at No. 31 occupied the site of the former Bakers Temperance Hotel (est. 1874) but in the early 1930s the hotel moved to Ivy Lane and is now known as the Chaucer Hotel. At this time the building was renamed Parade Chambers and provided accommodation for a number of offices, small businesses and a tea room. Parade Chambers, too, was destroyed by the bombing of 1942. Later, the Barretts motor company occupied the premises formerly used by the Canterbury Club.

Barclays Bank at No. 23, which had only been built in 1920, was damaged but salvaged, its upper storeys being dismantled and a new roof built over the ground floor. It continued to operate like this for around six years but was eventually taken down in 1953. A new bank was erected on the same site and was operating by 1955. The street was renumbered and the bank was now at No. 9. The National Provincial Bank at No. 25 had also been damaged and was demolished. In 1956, a new bank was constructed on its foundation, becoming No. 7.

At No. 24 was a grocers called World's Stores and at No. 22 Dolcis, the shoe shop. By the end of 1955, Dolcis was trading in new premises at No. 13 and the new No. 11 was occupied by James Walker Jewellers.

The Marks & Spencer store at Nos 30-34, which dated from the 1930s, survived the raid and the fine Regency-style frontage dominated the street. After the raid, the building was surrounded by bombed sites but an extension of the shop was subsequently built adjoining the original building. The new road plan, Holden's Plan, provided for the Civic Way to pass by the Marks & Spencer premises but this was eventually abandoned.

At No. 39, east of Marks & Spencer, was a single-storey printing works used by the *Kentish Gazette* and, after the Blitz, wooden sheds were put up to accommodate the equipment. People recall that the ruined St George's Street was covered in elder and buddleia in the late

1940s. Amid the shrubs and trees, wooden signs sprouted up to notify the public about the relocation of companies that had traded there. One announced that E. Bing & Son, (Savory and Moore) had removed to Sun Street, while another stated that 'Mac Fisheries have transferred the business, formerly carried on at No. 42 St George's Street, to No. 2 Lower Bridge Street, Canterbury'.

The Coach and Horses public house, just beyond the St George's Lane junction, was also abandoned and a sign left to tell passers-by that they had moved to No. 1 Guildhall Street, where they remained until the 1950s. They were able to return following the redevelopment and their new street number was No. 32. The original cellars of Jay's Furnishing Stores and the Coach and Horses are now beneath the widened main street.

After the bombing in 1942 until the redevelopment in the 1950s, there was an excellent opportunity to research Canterbury's past, particularly its Roman origins. The east wall of a cellar beneath the former premises of the stationer's WHSmith & Son was found to be Roman. Further investigations unearthed a Roman bathhouse in four cellars that extended along the frontage occupied today by WHSmith and Woolworths.

St George's Street in the 1950s looked very different from today. Pat Griffin remembers visiting Canterbury in 1956. 'Most of the shops, including WHSmith, were still in prefabricated buildings', she says.

Number 24, on the corner of St George's Street and Canterbury Lane, is a Superdrug store today but was occupied by David Greig's shop, which sold meat, fish and cheese, in the 1950s. This was a stunningly modern development, designed by Robert Paine & Partners and completed in 1953. The building's design, which is thought to have been influenced by the

Superdrug on the corner St George's Street and Canterbury Lane.

Above and left: Work on the Whitefriars development, summer 2004.

1951 Festival of Britain, was awarded a Royal Institute of British Architects bronze medal in 1956. The shop closed down in the late 1970s.

Perry Johnson worked at David Greig's as a Saturday boy to save up for a moped. The supervisor's son, who was the school bully, also worked as a Saturday boy. One day, he challenged Perry about the fact that he had taken a Saturday off and Perry punched him on the nose. Perry was cheered by the other boys at school for punching the bully but was sacked when he turned up for work the following Saturday.

A new Woolworths store opened in July 1952 on the north side of the street. It was a typical 1950s construction of red brick over a steel frame, with a flat roof in the modernist style. The foundations of a blitzed building were laid out in the cellar. This was the first new development in the street after the bomb damage and people were immediately attracted to the three wide window displays. On Friday 25 January 1952, a long queue awaited the opening of the doors and when they got inside, it was too crowded for people to buy anything!

In 1951, the year of the Festival of Britain, an exhibition was held from 11 June to 12 September to demonstrate the city's historical heritage. There were exhibits covering themes such as: The Iron Age, The Romans, Christianity, Thomas Becket and Pilgrimages, as well as more modern concerns such as Agriculture and The Blitz, Today and Tomorrow. Stanley Jennings, who had been elected Mayor of Canterbury in May 1949 and received an OBE in the 1952 New Year's Honours List for his services to the Canterbury Festival, was involved

Right: Boots chemists, facing the bus station.

Below: The Buddleia Years describes the period after the Second World War, when the plant grew on bombed sites everywhere. A present reminder on waste ground opposite Fenwick's.

in the exhibition and helped to clear the St George's Street site. When the exhibition closed down, the site was redeveloped.

The redevelopment programme for St George's Street was nearing its end in 1959. Impressive frontages included the National Provincial Bank and the adjacent Barclays Bank. In 1961, the Co-op moved from Lower Bridge Street to new premises, Marlowe House, on the north side of St George's Street. These premises were formerly a theatre and the Co-op extended them at the rear and along Burgate Lane. Later, C & A occupied the building, then Wilkinsons.

Today, St George's Street is pedestrianised and the huge Fenwick store now occupies the site that was occupied by Canterbury's first supermarket, Price Rite, and then Riceman's department store prior to the Whitefriars development.

St George's Terrace

St George's Terrace once ran along the rear of the city wall, just above where the bus station now stands. This is the high point from which people used to view the goings-on in the cattle market below in Upper Bridge Street.

The Sun Building, with its tall, pitched roof and its ivy-covered frontage, stood on the corner of St George's Terrace and St George's Street during the 1930s but was destroyed in the Blitz. Adjoining buildings occupying prime positions along the raised terrace were Martin's the drapers and the Halifax building society.

During the 1940s, religious ceremonies were held by pilgrims on St George's Terrace. Part of the street was bombed in June 1942. Ruth Taylor, who lived in Cossington Road, was on ambulance duty at the time and saw an entire terrace of three-storey houses turn into a sheet of flame that seemed to disappear into the sky. After the bombing, a fence was erected so that people didn't fall over the edge. The remaining houses were demolished later the same year and now nothing remains of the original street.

St Margaret's Street

St Margaret's Street runs from Watling Street to the High Street and was named after St Margaret's church, which is now home to the Canterbury Tales visitor attraction. 'West's animated coloured pictures' were shown at St Margaret's Hall on Boxing Day, 1903. Entrepreneurs Robert and Lloyd Forsyth, who were responsible for the Victoria Pier in Folkestone, rented the larger of the two halls situated in St Margaret's Street from 8 November 1909 to use as a picture palace. In February 1911, William Henry Court, of the furniture business, formed Electric Picture Palace (Canterbury) Ltd, but competition from the Canterbury Electric theatre in St Peter's Street prevented the venture from becoming viable and films were dropped. The hall was used as a YMCA from December 1914 and then as the Empire Music Hall until its demolition in 1926.

It was replaced by the Central Picture Theatre, designed by H. Anderson in the Tudor

Above left: An opening for archers in the city wall now provides a view over Upper Bridge Street.
Above right: A woodcarving at No. 28a St Margaret's Street. *(Copyright Stephen Bax)*

style, with casement windows. This cinema seated 735 people, an impressive number for the time. The first film shown was *The Somme* on 7 November 1927. In September, 1935, the Central Picture Theatre became an ABC cinema. It was bombed twice during the war and was forced to close for five months. It reopened on 22 March 1943, continued to operate until September 1948, when it was bought for £20,000 by the city council and converted into a theatre. This was the original Marlowe Theatre, which opened on 19 May 1950 with *The Chiltern Hundreds*. The Marlowe continued to entertain the crowds with plays, shows and revues, including a performance by Mary O'Hara, the celebrated singer, on 22 May 1982, until the building was demolished and replaced by a shopping complex. The new Marlowe Theatre is to be found in The Friars.

The car park adjoining the Marlowe Theatre was the place where people gathered to sing carols every year during the 1960s. The service was often attended by the archbishop, who, in 1961, was Michael Ramsey.

In the twentieth century, St Margaret's Street contained Canterbury's largest and most important grocer's, the family business Frederick Finn & Son. Their premises were at No. 21 and were run in the 1920s by two brothers, Raymond and Percy. The shop had a sign advertising 'Finn's Stores Café for Luncheons and Teas. Comfortably Furnished Tea and Smoking Rooms reached either by Stairs or Electric Lift'. Finn's were famous for the fine biscuits they stocked, including Huntley & Palmers, Peek Freans and McVitie Price, and made deliveries to their customers using errand boys.

In the late 1940s, F.N. Nason, hotel furnishers, took over part of the premises previously occupied by Finns, while Lewis Chiropodists were at No. 19, the Pilgrim's Tea House at No. 20, and Walpamur Co. Paint Manufacturers at No. 21. On the opposite side of the road were the North Sea Fish Company at No. 29a, George Mount Florists at No. 29b and the London Outfitters at No. 30. The premises of Hunt, Snell & Co., printers, at No. 18 were destroyed in 1942.

Number 36, at the junction with Hawks Lane, was occupied by B.C. Blyth & Son, wine merchants. It was the site at the centre of the old Roman town, probably dating from the late first or early second century, according to evidence uncovered during the digging of a pit for a new lift shaft. This exciting find included clay flooring, decomposed timber planks and late first-century pottery. The off-licence, Threshers, now occupies the site.

The Royal Fountain Hotel was completely destroyed in the Blitz. Dating from 1029, it was the oldest public house in Kent, possibly in the whole of England. Princess Victoria was a guest on 10 August 1835, according to *The Gazette*, which described the elegance of the young ladies who gathered there. The hotel was important enough to justify alteration to the nearby St Margaret's church, whose stone façade impeded the horse-driven coaches when they tried to turn to go through the hotel's gate. The space caused by its destruction was filled by the Marlowe Arcade shopping development.

After the destruction caused in the Blitz, a relief road was planned across the city from east to west. Damaged buildings were to be sacrificed to make space for it, among them the Freemasons' Tavern in St Margaret's Street. In 1965, it looked tipsier than its occupants, since it was lopsided and part of the roof was covered in corrugated iron. This was due to the bomb damage which had disposed of half of the building. It was pulled down, along with some other buildings, but the promised relief road did not materialise.

St Martin's Terrace

The houses on this terrace were built for prison officers and date from the early twentieth century, with mock-Tudor gables.

St Mary's Street

St Mary's Street, which runs from Castle Street to Marlowe Avenue, was once a drain for the medieval city of Canterbury.

It's hard to believe that lovely St Mary's Street was once a drain, 2004.

St Peter's Lane

The White House, situated on the right if approaching from St Peter's Street, is said to have been the retirement home of Queen Victoria's head coachman. Next door stands the Red House, an equally grand, brick-built structure.

During the Second World War, the 3rd (Canterbury) Battalion Home Guard used the Drill Hall. A recruitment poster proclaimed:

> 3rd (Canterbury) BN, HOME GUARD, If interested in joining get
> the official card at any Post office or enrol at DRILL HALL, St Peter's
> Lane, Canterbury. Your Liberty is worth Preserving. Be Prepared.

Kent Batallions were always given a number and Canterbury's St Augustine's Batallion had the numbers 3rd and 4th. Canterbury was defended by both the Home Guard and the Army based at Howe Barracks.

St Peter's Place

The close proximity of St Peter's Place to the River Stour exposed it to flooding. October 1909 was particularly bad and many roads in the area were affected. Holy Cross and St Peter's School at the end of the road had to be closed down, much to the delight of the local schoolchildren. During the Second World War, there was a public air-raid shelter in St Peter's Place.

The old East Kent bus station was the final destination of the No. 8 double-decker bus from Margate. Nowadays, the bus turns in the opposite direction at the junction between the High Street and Guildhall. Back in the 1950s, the roads were full of buses and bicycles rather than cars.

At the top end of St Peter's Place was a row of houses, Nos 1–8 Camden Terrace, built of Victorian redbrick, which dated from the 1880s. They were demolished when the St Peter's roundabout was built in 1962. The new dual carriageway crossed over the old city wall, connecting St Peter's Place to Wincheap Green.

On the left when approaching the roundabout is a community drop-in centre for people with mental illness, or for anyone in times of loneliness or distress, known as the Canterbury Umbrella. 'There is always someone to talk to at Umbrella,' is the charity's motto. The centre was started in 1985 in the old Methodist church hall in St Peter's Street and moved to its present site seven years later. Manager Sally Stace, who started as a volunteer many years ago, says that the centre meets the needs of people no longer accommodated by psychiatric hospitals such as St Augustine's, who have to manage on their own in the community. Volunteers provide such diverse services as counselling, reflexology, computer training and keep fit.

Holy Cross and St Peters School was demolished in the 1970s. At one time, the school owned a prefab on the site of the Umbrella centre.

St Peter's Street

St Peter's Street crosses the River Stour at King's Bridge. In the early twentieth century, the Canterbury Post Office Authority purchased the large house of Mr Alfred Neame for conversion into a post office here.

To the left, along the river bank, is a row of medieval houses, known as the Weavers' Houses, which date from the sixteenth century, when Huguenot and Walloon weavers plied their trade, having fled their own countries to escape persecution. The houses, which are now used as shops and restaurants have been fully restored and have twentieth-century beams on their outside façades.

A grisly relic of medieval times is the ducking stool which hangs over the river. It was used to see if women accused of witchcraft were guilty or not. If the accused survived, she was a witch and was burned; if she drowned, she was innocent. In this age, Canterbury's swans did not enjoy the protection they do today. They were deliberately fattened for banquets and, as the river was often used as a public lavatory, some of the poor birds died from pollution. This was not a good time to be a swan or a woman with a third nipple!

In 1807, James Callaway, the traditional producer of fine silks and Canterbury muslin, died and, as a result, many of Canterbury's silk mills were closed down. In 1899, Miss C.F. Philpotts and Miss K. Holmes restored the craft of weaving to the area by moving into the old weaver's house, formerly used by Callaway, opposite King's Bridge.

The foundation for the Masonic Temple was laid on 4 March 1880. The temple, situated on the corner of St Peter's Place, near Westgate, was designed by John Green Hall, who was

A view of the old Westgate.

the city surveyor. Many Lodges and Chapters have met at the Temple over the years.

Canterbury's eminent artist, Thomas Sidney Cooper, specialised in paintings of cattle and sheep. He spent his early life in a cottage in St Peter's Street, living in near poverty because his father deserted the family, leaving his mother to bring up five children by herself. Mrs Cooper earned her living by dressmaking and managed to raise two eminent sons in these difficult circumstances. While Thomas became a Royal Academy artist, from whom both Queen Victoria and Edward VII purchased pictures, another Cooper son became the mayor of Canterbury. T.S. Cooper bought the cottage and founded the art school next door, the purpose of which was to encourage new talent and provide facilities that had not been available to the young Thomas. It now houses the Chaucer Centre and community halls and is easy to recognise by its impressive portico. Cooper dedicated the art school to his mother's memory in 1867 and continued his philanthropic acts towards his native city.

Mary Tourtel, creator of Rupert Bear, was trained at the Sidney Cooper School of Art. There is a statue of Rupert Bear, in his distinctive yellow trousers and scarf and red pullover, at the Canterbury Heritage Museum, and a road is named for her.

St Peter's Methodist church dates from 1811 and is noted for the symmetry of its construction. Another fine building is No. 13, which was built around 1600 and has beautiful carvings and low windows.

Above left: A street musician outside St Peter's Methodist church, 2004.
Above right: Number 41 St Peter's Street, from a painting presented as a gift to owner Michel Piquet.
(Copyright Michel Piquet)

The photographer Henry B. Collins moved from his St George's Street premises to No. 33 in 1894, where he continued in business until the First World War. At this point, Ackland and Youngman took over Henry's studio.

During the First World War, the Dutch Tea House began trading from No. 24, next door to the art school. The Tea House charged 1s 6d for lunch. Between 4 p.m. and 6 p.m., people went there to enjoy the sumptuous interior and listen to music. It ceased trading in 1958 or 1959.

The little Café St Pierre at No. 41, on the corner of St Peter's Street and Black Griffin Lane, has known many changes. Since the Second World War, it has traded as a tobacconist's, a building society, an estate agent and a bakery and café. The building still displays evidence that it was a bakery, as 'Hanry bread' and 'Biscuit Baker' can be seen on the façade. The 1930s-style bakerman design, complete with its tall white hat, wraps around two sides of the building. Now, it is run by proprietor Michel Piquet as a café once more. French-born Michel came to England twenty years ago to study our language and liked England so much he decided to stay. He took over Café St Pierre in the summer of 1995 and the business is now a popular focal point for Canterbury residents and tourists alike.

Number 43 is another medieval dwelling, built around 1600, while No. 46 housed F.C. Snell's picture-framing business from just after the First World War until the late 1930s. After the Second World War, the World Stores Ltd grocers moved into the property.

The Canterbury Electric picture palace, designed by F.H. Dore and A.R. Bowles, opened at No. 49a on 1 June 1911, announcing, 'If our programme pleases, tell your friends; if not, the manager.' This early cinema had a glass canopy over the entrance and a central paybox and could accommodate 520 people on modern tip-up seats. It was carpeted in plush red and had silk lampshades. It closed on 5 November 1927 and was later changed into the Odeon Music Hall, then became the Canterbury Repertory Theatre on 31 August 1936. At the end of the war, this old picture palace became a restaurant, Perry's Talisman, frequented by boys from King's School but, more recently, the restaurant has served Chinese food as the Lok Yin.

The Odeon ballroom in St Peter's Street boasted a resident band, Frederic Hargreaves and his Swingtette, from 1942 to the 1960s. The entrance fee during the war years was 1s on slow nights and 2s on more popular nights. The Talisman ballroom was popular during the 1950s. Ken Grieff led the band, which included two brothers, George and Tony Coe, who played the clarinet. Tony Coe, who once attended the Simon Langton Boys' School, was awarded an honorary Doctor of Music degree in 1988 from the University of Kent.

In 1905, No. 27 was leased to Mr Barrett for £63 a year and bicycles, sports and camping equipment were sold from the premises. Later, George Barrett took up agencies for Ford and Rover cars and also introduced a Rover taxi service to compete with the horse-drawn carriages already in existence. Sid Baker, an employee of the business since 1902, was the first taxi driver, and he continued until his retirement in 1958. George Barrett was married to Florence Cobbett and they had three children, Elsie, John and Reginald. The two sons became active in the business.

The motor garage of G.R. Barrett was established in 1902 and occupied 26 St Peter's Street. In 1904, No. 30 was acquired and in 1931 Nos. 28 and 29 also became part of Barrett's motor business. At one time, prior to 1914, it was possible to hire a taxi from the garage and the fare was one shilling a mile. Mr Barrett acquired an agency for Rover cars in 1904 and became mayor in 1927. In 1909 a small showroom was built on the corner of St Peter's Street and Pound Lane. During the Second World War, Barrett's took part in a campaign with the Kentish Gazette to raise funds to buy a Spitfire. In the garage, they displayed a Messerschmitt that had crash landed and they managed to raise £88.0s. 1d for the fund. In 1938 a new, purpose-built garage appeared on the site although this was destroyed during an enemy air raid during January 1944. Apparently there are still charred remnants from the tall building embedded in the party wall to the next door building. During the 1940s and '50s, on the corner of St Peter's Street and St Peter's Place, was the Seeboard showroom, which was formerly the Corner House café. Beyond these buildings stood the white-rendered premises of F.G. Cornfoot the chemists.

Although buildings were demolished at the west end of St Peter's Street, road plans were dropped and the proposed ring road did not materialise. As a result, Barretts returned to the area in the late 1970s and still trade on this prime site today.

Premises now named Welby's Bazaar after the former owners, wine merchants Welby & Co. were, prior to 1969, called the Oporto Tavern, whose proprietor from the mid-1930s to the mid-1950s was Mr William Francis White. He was a portly gentleman who liked his pipe, as is suggested by the postcard sporting his likeness which he gave away to his customers.

Woolworths had occupied Nos 47-48 until 1952. When,they relocated to new premises in St George's Street, the building was converted into two separate shops, Frank's and Sixty Minute Cleaners Ltd. The two timber-framed shops suffered a small fire in their shared roof and were demolished, together with neighbouring Longley's butcher shop. At this time, it seems that any excuse was used to demolish, in order to replace nineteenth-century buildings with new shop premises.

The impressive Cogan House, a twelfth-century building with two-foot thick Norman stone walls, was the home of Canterbury's mayors and bailiffs and has a twelfth-century aisled timber hall and Tudor panelling. Nowadays, it is used as a restaurant.

St Radigund's Street

St Radigund's Street was named for the monks of St Radigund at Bradsole (known in early medieval times as Froxpole), near Dover and the enormous house of the abbot of St Radigund's once stood here.

St Radigund's Street was once named Waterlock Lane after the bridge over the river, which was a watergate and therefore locked in the water. In 1800, a new bridge crossed the Stour, probably to accommodate foot passengers. It was known as Long Bridge and extended across both stream and river. In 1821, a brick, arched bridge was built over Mill Street for horses and carts but these vehicles had to negotiate the river itself by means of a ford. In 1843, a bridge was built which crossed both stream and river.

In the nineteenth century, Abbot's Mill stood in St Radigund's Street, so-called because an earlier mill was owned by the abbey. During the 1890s, it was purchased by Thomas Denne from Sidney Cooper and was rechristened Denne's Mill. On 17 October 1933, a huge fire destroyed the mill, which was originally built in 1792. The fire was reported as starting in the hayloft around 8.30 a.m. and the inferno swiftly extended to the Miller's Arms public house and the street, where people were watching from the bridge area. Fire engines came from Canterbury, Bridge, Sturry and Herne Bay.

Mr and Mrs Lilley lived at No. 13 with their daughter and a land girl called Mary, who slept in the back bedroom. Mr Lilley was employed by the electricity works. Like other homes in the street, the house was threatened during the raids and the occupants took cover in the shelter and under the shored-up stairway. Mr Lilley stayed outside and reassured himself by keeping an eye on the chimney pot because all the time it was still standing, he knew his loved ones were all right. They were all very relieved to have come through the ordeal unhurt.

The St Radigund's baths once occupied a plot behind the Dolphin, where the car park is now. In 1794, a stretch of the city wall was demolished to allow a new road

Simple Simon's in Church Lane, off St Radigund's Street.

A detail of Simple Simon's.

to be built to the baths, which was descibed as 'a fine spring built over and fitted for cold bathing'.

The Simple Simon's public house is a timber-framed building dating from the fifteenth century and, although strictly speaking its address is Nos 3-9 Church Lane, it is situated in a tiny slip road running behind St Radigund's Gardens. In the 1930s, the building was condemned as unfit for human habitation and developers started to pull down the eighteenth-century façade, discovering two Kent hall houses, built between 1350 and 1450. Evidence suggested that, during the eighteenth century, two pubs traded from the site, which was considerably extended on one side. Although reports conflict, it does appear that at one time a row of seven tumbledown cottages may have existed here. The building was used as a dance hall in around 1933, then a youth club and it has also served as part of the Art and Design faculty for Christ Church College. More recently, it was Radigund's Diner. The present landlord, Michael Patten, bought the premises in 1983 and it opened in 1987 as a public house proud of its 'real ales and real cider,' as well as its great jazz, blues and folk music.

Bligh's engineering works once traded in the area now designated as St Radigund's Gardens and stands in front of Simple Simon's. Sometimes, on the garage forecourt, could be seen one of the original cars that were the inspiration for *Chitty Chitty Bang Bang*. Count Zborowski, who lived in a fine stately home at Bridge, just outside Canterbury, drove around the streets of Canterbury in Chitty 1, a chain-driven, lengthened Mercedes built in 1921. Altogether, the count, who was the son of a Polish count and an American mother, named three of his racing cars Chitty. He was killed in around 1925, while racing in the Italian Grand Prix.

In the late eighteenth and early nineteenth century, 5,000 troops, both infantry and artillery, were housed in barracks in this area of the city. The area was so dangerous that police patrolled in pairs. The St Radigund's Gardens were created by the City Council in 1978 and 1979, and presented to the city.

Many early nineteenth-century terraces were sacrificed here for the proposed third stage of the ring road. The demolition was described as slum clearance. The road scheme was finally cancelled and the area was replaced by a number of car parks. Towards 1966, most properties were empty, although Mr D. Gebbie lived at No. 4, while Miss O. Emery remained at No. 6.

View from an upstairs window in Simple Simon's, showing a modern end-of-terrace house in Duck Lane next to a Victorian end-terrace in St Radigund's Street.

Pat giving children swimming lessons at Beauherne Primary School. The pool was halfway between the infants' and juniors'.
(Copyright Pat Griffin)

The old signal box at Station Road East.

Station Road East

Station Road East was built in 1860 to serve the stations for London, Chatham and Dover. According to the ladies of the early twentieth century, one of the best things about Station Road was the hat shop, which was willing to let a lady take away six hats to try on approval. Opposite, Mr Durtnell sold women's clothing, underclothes and elastic. He was much in demand for wedding and evening dresses and for christening gowns.

Cadbury Bros owned premises here and the manager during the early 1930s was Albert Bailey. The building now houses a snooker club.

Station Road West

Station Road West, built in 1846, was one of several on the New North Kent Line of the South Eastern Railway serving Ashford to Margate. It contained a terrace of eight cottages, Station Cottages, built around the same period to house railway and coal yard workers. In March 1974, squatters were evicted from No. 3, after displaying a 'Homes for people, not for profit' banner. When the police arrived, there seemed to be around seven young people in residence, six girls and a boy. Everyone was smiling! It seems the Canterbury spirit survives during good times and bad!

Today, a point of interest in this area is the refurbished Victorian railway goods shed, which was originally used to store coal coming into the city. Situated just outside Canterbury West station, it provides a daily farmers' market, food hall and restaurant. The market operates from Tuesday to Sunday and has more than seventeen stalls for local farmers to display their produce and deal directly with the public. The farmers' publicity reads: 'An enticing range of breads, home-made cakes and savouries, shellfish, cheese, organic meat and eggs, as well as organic fruits and vegetables. Unique to Canterbury, the Farmers' Market also has a restaurant, The Goods Shed, boasting a menu that changes twice daily to reflect the best seasonal produce available. Food is prepared by top London chef, Blaise Vasseur, using produce directly from the market.' The market is popular for those who like to support local farmers and growers and who prefer fresh foods that are insecticide-free and organic. Also, there is free-range meat from local livestock farmers, including Chandler and Dunn, who own a cattle herd in Ash. Nash Organic Nurseries provide fine vegetables such as courgettes.

Stone Street

This old Roman road runs from Canterbury to Hythe and it is here, in Lime Tree Farmhouse, that Mr and Mrs Thornton lived with their children, Penelope, Peggy, Philip, Phoebe and Christopher (Kit). An uncle from Liverpool would fly down to Canterbury to visit the Thorntons, landing his craft on a field near to the farmhouse. Towards the end of August 1939, an anti-aircraft unit arrived on Stone Street and Mr Thornton helped the searchlight party rig up their Lewis gun and also arranged for one sapper to stay in their house in case there was an urgent telephone call. During the war, Penelope became a nurse while Peggy joined the

The young Thorntons of Stone Street in 1941. From left to right: Penelope, Peggy, Christopher, Phoebe and Philip. *(Courtesy of Peggy Poole)*

WRNS and Phoebe served in the Land Army. Philip Thornton volunteered as a soldier, joining the Buffs (the Royal East Kent Regiment). In 1941, he left from Canterbury East station for his posting in India. He then went off to fight in Burma, where he was killed at Donbaik in 1943. Philip loved music and had often sung at carol concerts, giving performances which prompted one old man to say, 'I thought I heard the angels sing last night'. After his death, his parents received a letter from complete strangers in India (where he had been training for a year on tanks) which said, 'As long as Christmas has its carols, we shall remember your son.' Philip Thornton's name is inscribed on the war memorial in the Buttermarket.

The family left the farm in 1946 and it is now a Grade II listed building. The youngest member of the family, Christopher, known as Kit, became chairman of the Kent County Council in June 2001 and now lives in Sevenoaks.

Stour Street

Stour Street, originally named Lamb Lane, is situated off St Dunstan's Street and the river runs parallel with it. Water Lane runs off it towards the Stour, while what was once another Water Lane nearby has now been renamed Linden Grove. Stour Street provided an entrance to the rear of the post office situated on the King's Bridge, to provide access for the mail carts and avoid disrupting traffic in the street.

E. Beasley, dyers and cleaners, at Nos 22-24 were established in 1806 but the premises were destroyed in June 1942. Reportedly, only one high-explosive bomb fell on Stour Street but it did much damage around the junction with Beer Cart Lane. The damaged buildings were demolished but Beasley's managed to carry on by hanging a sign on their door redirecting customers to the Presbyterian Hall, where they dealt with enquiries. The bombs completely destroyed the Weights and Measures Office.

The most impressive building in this street is the Poor Priests' Hospital, whose chequered history began in 1218, when it was founded by Alexander of Gloucester for poor, elderly or sick priests. The hospital was closed during the reign of Elizabeth I and the priests finally vacated in 1575. Since then, it has served a number of purposes, including a house of correction and a school. Before the Second World War, it was partly occupied by F.H. Browne & Sons, organ builders.

The Poor Priests' Hospital received only minor damage to the roof in 1942 and this was subsequently repaired. During the war, the front area was used as an ambulance station and, in addition to becoming the headquarters of the St John's Ambulance Brigade, by 1946 it also housed St John's Medical Comfort Depot and the Canterbury Health Department. The hospital was also used as an antenatal clinic for some time, and has served as the Buffs Regimental Museum. Since 1987, it has been the Heritage Museum for the city of Canterbury. There have also been many material changes to the hospital during its colourful history. For example, during its restoration in the 1970s and '80s, some post-medieval additions such as dormer windows and chimney stacks were removed. It was at this time that

The old tannery at Stour Street, 2004.

the foundations of a stone house were discovered, which proved it was the home of Lambin Frese, a coin minter, in 1174 and was taken over by Adam of Charing in 1180. The latter died in 1207 and Lambin's son, Roger, moved back in.

Road improvements threatened Stour Street until the 1970s. One proposal was to widen it as an access road for a lorry-unloading area near Jewry Lane. People called this the Stour Street motorway. Fortunately, the road plan never materialised and the street remained residential.

Opposite the Poor Priests' Hospital is a modern business centre named The Old Brewery.

The Great Stour Brewery and Museum is at No. 75, and visitors are encouraged to make their own beer in their miniature facsimile of a commercial brewery.

Adjacent to the Poor Priests' Hospital, Trev's Cycles (formerly Cycle Mart) traded for eleven years, but has now been taken over by Tribb's Cycles.

Nowadays, tourists take rides around the city in a horse and carriage, starting from Stour Street.

At the end of Stour Street, at its junction with Rosemary Lane, stands St Mildred's Tannery, whose outbuildings, now derelict, extended behind as far as the River Stour and Rheims Way. The old tannery is to be demolished shortly to provide 444 houses and flats, a car park, a hotel, several shops and a restaurant.

Sun Street

This little street, which connects the Buttermarket with Palace Street, was originally home to medieval rush markets and is named after the sixteenth-century Sun Hotel. The Sun Hotel is the site of Mr Micawber's rooms in *David Copperfield*.

After being bombed in June 1942, the greengrocer's, David Greig at Nos 12-13 St George's Street needed new premises and relocated to Nos 19-21 Sun Street, where they remained until a new shop was opened at No. 23 St George Street in 1953. The manager at their Sun

Above left: Street signs on the corner of Sun and Guildhall Streets, 2004.
Above right: Detail of the upper storeys of the former Sun Hotel. (Copyright Stephen Bax)

Street shop in the late 1940s was Bill Rigden. Another business that moved from a blitzed St George's Street address was E. Bing & Son (Savory & Moore Ltd.), who were chemists.

In 1875, William and Frances Lefevre arrived in Canterbury and started a draper's shop in Sun Street. William's father had previously owned a greengrocer's in Military Road. Mr and Mrs Lefevre produced fifteen children and the youngest child, Charles, inherited the business from his father. He became an important city personage and was elected mayor in 1937. By this time, the status of the Lefevre family name was firmly established.

There was a scandal in Sun Street in the early 1960s when Mr Woods opened his butcher's shop. The shop was popular and people queued to purchase his fine turkeys at Christmas but when Mr Woods received a visit from an inspector, the sausages were discovered to be dusty and dirty. Mr Woods was furious, complaining that his hygiene was exemplary; after all, he had another shop on the south coast with a fine reputation. In an article in the newspaper, he claimed that a member of his staff must have betrayed him by deliberately contaminating the sausages. Finally, some time in the late 1970s, a disenchanted Mr Woods closed up his formerly successful butcher's shop.

Outside the jeweller's and silversmith's, T & B Cousins & Sons at Nos 8, 9 and 9a, hangs a wall sign proclaiming that the building was originally the Sun Hotel, constructed in 1503. Prior to this, it was the Little Inn. T & B Cousins & Sons is a family firm founded in 1920. It has been run by three generations of the Cousins family, selling, repairing, restoring, re-polishing and re-cutting precious gemstones. The building itself was restored by Debenhams in 1992.

On the corner of Sun Street and Guildhall Street is Deakin's, a family business now in its 149th year.

T

Turnagain Lane

Aptly named because it goes nowhere, Turnagain Lane is nevertheless a fascinating cul-de-sac. On the right is a row of three-storey houses, with jettied middle storeys. Further down is a newer house called Whittington House.

U

Union Street

Union Street was widened after the slum clearance of early nineteenth-century houses on the north side of the street in 1959 and became a main access route from the Sturry Road into Canterbury.

The William IV public house dates from the early eighteenth century and can be found close to the turning with Victoria Row. It was one of the buildings to survive full-scale demolition in 1962. The Union Castle, however, was sacrificed to the clearance scheme, as were a row of early nineteenth-century terraces on the south side of the street. Architect John Berbiers designed blocks of maisonettes in March 1968, which were erected on the cleared site. Most of the buildings in Union Street are now in the modern style.

The garage of P.D. Tobin Ltd was completed in the early 1960s and stood on the corner between Union Street and Union Place.

Upper Bridge Street

Before the Second World War, the cattle market functioned on land between the city walls and Upper Bridge Street, which is now part of the ring road. This area was once a moat!

Animals were always being driven through the town and one character who is well-remembered in Canterbury is Milky Willis, who took his pigs to the market with their legs tethered with a piece of string. Milky Willis had a big beard and a hard hat.It was often chaotic, with animals escaping and people having to take action to avoid being run down. Drovers hired themselves out to farmers for about 6d and one man regularly drove 200 sheep, with the help of his dog, along what is now the A2 from Bridge to the cattle market. Farmer's son Dudley Pout regarded trips to Canterbury as a special day out. One day, he and his father drove fifteen bullocks to the market, setting off at 5.30 a.m. It was Dudley's job, as the youngest drover, to go ahead and open and close gates.Once the animals reached market, they were held in wooden pens.

The beautiful Georgian and Regency background to the market changed dramatically after the Blitz, as the attractive terrace houses that overlooked the market from St George's Terrace were lost.

Close to the St George's crossroads, near to the premises of G. Twyman, a section of the market was used as a car park. After 1955, the car park ran along the entire strip, as a new cattle market had been built in Market Way, now Dover Street.

There was a less savoury aspect to the cattle market during the first part of the nineteenth century because markets were sometimes used, in Canterbury and elsewhere, for men to sell their wives, often their children as well. It is said that 10s was paid for a wife and two children on one occasion. Sometimes the wives were actually glad to be sold!

People enjoyed watching the comings and goings from St George's Terrace, which overlooked the market, and it must have been a good day out at the weekend, with the Salvation Army playing and singing on Saturdays and Sundays.

There were a number of auctioneer's premises around the area of the cattle market, dating from the nineteenth century. Their premises were actually cut into the city wall and the bank behind the wall and St George's Terrace ran above them. Included among these auctioneers were Auto Auctions of Canterbury, who sold cars, commercial vehicles and motor bikes on Wednesdays. A distinctive artefact in the middle of the cattle market was the old weighing machine, which disappeared in the 1950s. The cattle market itself closed in 1955.

Upper Bridge Street suffered during the Blitz. The Co-op received a direct hit through the roof and the interior was badly damaged. It remained standing as its exterior walls were intact but the building was unsafe and had to be destroyed. Nos 4-9 were destroyed, although No. 3 survived. In the late 1940s, No. 3 was a dental surgery. Twyman's rope and twine store fell victim to the raid. It burned fiercely and there were 'blue flames all across the road', according to one spectator. Then there was an enormous bang and the entire building collapsed into the road.

In November 1965, construction began on a new, modern fire station on the east side of Upper Bridge Street, to replace the station in Old Dover Road. The architect for the new fire station, which opened in February 1967, was E.T. Ashley-Smith. Another striking development was Lombard House, a smart four-storey plate-glass structure of showrooms and offices, in front of which were the trees which surrounded the former cattle market. These came down when the second stage of the ring road was started.

Upper and Lower Chantry Lane

The lane's name came from the masses that were sung for the souls of the dead by priests in chantry chapels. The chapel in Chantry Lane was on the corner of Edward Road and was founded by a rich rector of St Paul's church in the thirteenth century.

Wartime fireman Eric Pettit recalled the Blitz in this part of town, describing how they 'got a pump and tried to save the buildings opposite the fire station on the corner of Chantry Lane. A high explosive bomb dropped beside us and threw a big gate on the fire engine. The fellow working the pumps was terribly shaken'. The fire Eric Pettit was trying to overcome was the one which destroyed the home of the Andrews family, located at No. 2 New Dover Road, on its corner with Lower Chantry Lane. (*see* New Dover Road.) Mr Pettit could actually hear the clusters of fire bombs dropping at regular intervals. The fire was immediately opposite Maltby's fire station and, unfortunately, the water mains received a direct hit so the firemen had to struggle with the water pressure. Eventually some pumps arrived from Folkestone and the water supply was drawn from the River Stour.

V

Vauxhall Road

Vauxhall Road is now largely industrialised but before the war it was an ordinary residential area. After the road was bombed, prefabs were built all along one side. This is where Brian and Verna Frisby spent their early childhood.

Mr Frisby spent six years of his life in a prisoner-of-war camp in Germany then, in 1946, he came home from the war and Brian was conceived, followed three years later by Verna. Verna's Polish name was due to her Mum hearing it mentioned on the radio and taking a fancy to it. The family had to live with grandmother Winifred, who once worked in an ammunition factory in Worcestershire, until the prefab was found for them in Canterbury. Verna recalls how her father, like many men, never mentioned what happened to him in the war because his experiences were too terrible to talk about. Verna attended St Peter's Methodist School and remembers the outside toilets and what fun it was to hide in them, out of sight of the teachers. Later, the family moved to the London Road estate. Verna married in the late 1960s, when she was eighteen, and the young couple bought a home at No. 98 Old Park Avenue, which cost £3150. Later, they moved to St Michael's Place and had two children, Darren in 1975 and Donna in 1978.

W

Watling Street

Prior to 1949, Watling Street passed under the Riding Gate bridge but the road near the Riding Gate was renamed the Old Dover Road. There are several suggestions as to how the Riding Gate earned its name, among them that it meant Red Gate or Rider's Gate, or even Reed Gate. It could even simply mean Road Gate.

St Andrew's United Reformed church, Watling Street, 2004.

At No. 1, the Inland Revenue occupied a large Georgian house, which was demolished in the early 1950s to allow for the construction of a bus station. No. 2 was another large house, in this case Victorian, which was occupied by a number of companies, among them W.E. Pinnock, removals and Frank Cooper, a builders' merchant.

Watling Street suffered badly in the raids of 1942. A Victorian Nonconformist chapel was badly damaged in a small raid in June 1942 and was hit again in the October raid. A temporary Congregational church was erected in 1949 to meet the community's needs while a proper replacement was built. The new church was built in the 1950s and was supposed to be permanent but was demolished in 2001. The temporary church was dismantled to provide Tyler Hill with a village hall. There were empty sites on either side of the church, where large houses had been damaged in the October raid and pulled down. Opposite, a row of properties, Nos 38-42, were demolished and that site became a surface car park.

Watling Chambers was occupied by the offices of the Clerk to the City Magistrates and the Public Analyst. The June 1942 air raids demolished the Chambers and many other buildings in Watling Street, and modern buildings now occupy the site. The United Reformed church, with its distinctive round dome, remained intact.

In 1966, the architect Anthony Mauduit received a Civic Trust Award for his skill in replacing properties lost in the Blitz with new developments that respected the older styles. A fine nineteenth-century house at No. 31 was undamaged while properties on either side were destroyed. It required a sensitive approach in order to combine the modernist style with older façades without spoiling the aesthetic overall quality of the area.

On the corner of Watling Street, at No. 15a, was the greengrocer's shop Brewer & Son. This Regency-style house, despite an early seventeenth-century wall, was pulled down to accommodate the widening of Rose Lane. No. 16 dates from around 1625.

At the junction of Watling Street and Marlowe Avenue, the Dane John Brewery stood until the early 1930s and then a new surface car park was provided on the site of the demolished brewery. In the Second World War, some Canterbury people, who had been made homeless by the air raids and had nowhere else to go, resorted to camping here.

At Nos 18-19 were two fine Dutch-gabled houses, which had been badly damaged internally in the Blitz. Their shells were allowed to remain until 1953 and, when they were finally demolished, they were almost completely covered in ivy. The site of the two houses became a large office block, white-rendered and built in the neo-Georgian style.

One of Canterbury's most unpopular constructions stood on a site between Watling Street and Gravel Walk: the multi-storey car park, built in 1969, whose ugliness repelled everyone. Thankfully, it was demolished to make way for the Whitefriars scheme.

Westgate Grove

Passing under the Westgate, the quaint and well-preserved Westgate Grove can be found to the right, running alongside the River Stour. From this point, Jeremy MacLeod and Greg Stobbs could be found running their boat trips.

Westgate Grove, a delightful street running parallel to the Stour, 2004

More pretty houses in Westgate Grove, 2004.

Above left: Jeremy MacLeod, who runs boat trips on the river, 2004.
Above right: Boats on the Stour by Westgate Grove, 2004.

Whitehall Road

Street names with the prefix 'white' often suggest a connection with the valuable salt trade and this lane may have provided a track across the East Kent peninsula for traders carrying salt. There was a swimming pool just off Whitehall Road, known as Toddlers Cove, which dated from 1876. The land was purchased by Alderman Frank Hookier in 1945 for the people of Canterbury but, due to health grounds, the pool was closed in the late 1960s. There had been a plan to construct a pool within Dane John, but this never happened and the Kingsmead Pool opened in 1971.

Whitehorse Lane

The name comes from a famous pub which used to be on the corner of the High Street and Whitehorse Lane. The lane was home to the Army Headquarters.

Beasley & Son dry-cleaner's was severely damaged in the 1942 bombing and their site was redeveloped in the 1960s. Five years later, No 5, an attractive mid-seventeenth-century house that was once the premises of George Snell the printer's, was demolished, as well as two adjacent eighteenth-century cottages, which also fell victim to the road-widening. The intention was for Whitehorse Lane to link the main street and relief road but, once again, the plans were never fully realised.

Whitstable Road

Whitstable Road is a long, mainly countrified, road from the seaside resort to Canterbury. A small business close to the St Dunstan's roundabout deserves a mention. This is a tiny post office and sweet shop and off-licence at Nos 21–23, freshly painted in bright turquoise by its owners, Louise and Colin Sanderson. They moved here from London two years ago, determined to succeed in business and they decided to make sure that their premises were impossible to miss! Louise says that, in around the 1920s, the premises belonged to Mr Shackleton. Older residents have described to Louise and Colin how people came for paraffin and were sent 'out back' with their jugs, bowls and containers to collect the fuel. Mr Shackleton also sold sweets and fruit and vegetables.

Old cottages near the St Dunstan's roundabout, 2004.

The St Dunstan's post office has a facelift, summer 2004.

Wincheap

The area around Wincheap was used by the Romans 2,000 years ago to grow vines for wine-making. Wincheap was established in around 1200 and was used for markets and fairs, due to the lack of space inside the city wall. Wincheap is said to derive from the Old English for wine market. However, there is an alternative suggestion, which is that it comes from weychep, derived from the Old English *waegnceap*, meaning a wagon. If this theory is right, wagons would have been bought and sold here and the road would have been wide enough for this.

At the top end of Wincheap was a fine Regency building called Woodville House, generally known as the Woodville Home for Children, whose matron was a Miss G.M. Pearson. Woodville House was demolished in 1957 and the area was laid out as a small road, Woodville Close, giving access to a development of flats.

Old photographs show the chimney of the Thanington water-pumping station facing Woodville House to its right. The pumping station was founded in 1879 and was finally removed in 2001 to make way for the huge Courts furnishing store. Courts had to pledge to build their new store in an identical style to the old building. The company went into liquidation in December 2004, shortly after their New Dover Road branch had been damaged by fire.

The Woodman's Arms public house ran a bat-and-trap team in the 1930s. It is said the game originated in the Canterbury area.

At No. 27, F.J. Clayson, 'Practical Watchmaker and Jeweller', started his business in 1908. Later, the business was taken over by his son, who continued until the late 1970s, and then the premises were occupied by Cico Stoves and Chimneys Ltd.

Before the First World War, the intriguingly-named Henry Bear's grocery store, which was 'noted for the finest provisions' was situated at No. 107 (old numbering). Henry Bear ran the shop in the early twentieth century and his son assisted him until the 1950s, when S.J. Kilby Ltd took it over. Number 107 was a grocer's until the 1980s, when it became a fish and chips restaurant. At some stage, it became No. 33. The new No. 107 was the Hop Poles public house, owned by Mackeson in the late 1940s. In 1950, the building was extended after the Thanington Dairy was demolished, and in the early twentieth century, the pub was rebuilt. At the time of writing, it stands empty with whitewashed windows.

The depot of Finn & Co., engineers and contractors, was at Seymour Place, Wincheap after the First World War. The driver at this time was William Beale, who married Winifred Best.

Orchard House at No. 173 was once a private school run by Miss Brothers. The ARP First Aid Party made it their headquarters at the beginning of the Second World War. Everyone connected with the ARP was a volunteer, apart from the man in charge, Mr Douglas Lye. They even had a Vauxhall car which they adapted so a stretcher could be accommodated. As a result, Orchard House became a sub-station to back up the main ambulance stations at the Poor Priests' Hospital in Stour Street, and two ambulances were parked in the garage there. Unfortunately, in October 1942, Orchard House was destroyed in the air raid, which also severely damaged nearby York Road. By a lucky chance, the First Aid post had been moved a few days previously. The site where Orchard House once stood now belongs to Sladdens, heating engineers.

Near to the junction of Wincheap and Castle Street stood two eighteenth-century houses, one of which was The Cedars. Both properties belonged to road contractors and hauliers C & G Yeoman and only the smaller one was residential. C & G Yeoman were well known in the city and, in addition, had business premises in Beer Cart Lane. They also occupied another building in Wincheap, now the Exhaust Centre. Up until the building of the 1963 ring road, C & G Yeoman remained in the larger of the two above-mentioned Georgian houses, having become part of the British Road Services in 1949. After the construction of the ring road, British Road Services made the best use they could of the reduced space, then Habitat took over the old depot.

The Georgian Thanington Hotel was once a farmhouse and is a Grade II listed building. It was built in around 1800 and a second floor was added thirty years later. A ten-roomed, purpose-built construction was completed in 1987 and linked by a conservatory to the main building, and in 1992 a swimming pool was installed.

Although it had survived the Wincheap roundabout project ten years earlier, St Andrew's Presbyterian church on Wincheap Green was demolished in March 1973. People had stopped worshipping at the church as early as the 1960s, although it was maintained for community amenities, for example, a youth club. Although another building behind the church was also sacrificed, the proposed development did not materialise. An interesting feature of the Wincheap roundabout is that it was once called Wincheap Green and was the site of a gallows.

Bluebells at No. 248 is a Victorian townhouse, now a guest house, which retains many of its original architectural features.

Courts had to build their new superstore in identical style to the old Thanington Pumping Station which formerly occupied the site, 2004.

Artist Bruce Williams painted the colourful images on an empty house, Wincheap, 2004.

The Crab and Winkle Way

I have included The Crab and Winkle Way in this book of Canterbury Streets, as it has been a very impoprtant landmark in the history of Canterbury. Not only was the original railway line used as a trade route, helping the fishermen of Whitstable to sell their wares in town, it also enabled ordinary Canterbury people in the past to spend a day (or more) enjoying the benefits of a holiday at the coast. Now the Crab and Winkle Way provides a footpath through beautiful countryside to the quaint fishing seaside town of Whitstable. It was part of the West station line but was closed after the Second World War, although traces of the past are still apparent on this famous footpath, which ramblers and students of the University of Kent still use today.

The Canterbury to Whitstable railway was the first locomotive passenger railway in the world. It opened on 4 May 1830, to the chiming of the cathedral's bells. An hourly service was run during daytime hours; ten trains each way, and it cost adults 9d and children 6d. The middle classes went on holiday to Tankerton and Whitstable and paid between 4d and 6d return for their holiday tickets. The famous *Invicta* locomotive was never actually used on the line. It was just for show, a mere tourist attraction and is now housed in the Canterbury Heritage Museum.

A tragedy occurred in 1909 at Tyler Hill, when a group of men working on the Whitstable railway were poisoned. The men were waiting for the key at the level crossing when one man, Setterfield, discovered a beer bottle. They all drank some of the beer but remarked that it tasted bitter. When they returned to their work, a man called Jordan complained of feeling ill. He collapsed and, within twenty minutes, was dead, leaving a widow, Beatrice, and four children. The other men also fell ill but eventually recovered. It was presumed that the bottle had been deliberately left close to the level crossing with the intention of poisoning the gateman, Noble. However, by the date of the resumption of the inquest, Monday 12 July, no further progress had been made through checks on chemists supplying strychnine. (Strychnine was often mixed with beer to fool animals that were to be poisoned.) An open verdict on this 'dastardly act' was recorded.

Opposite

Above: The old railway line, known as the Crab and Winkle Way. *(Copyright Canterbury Library Local Studies Collection, Kent County Council)*

Below: Aerial view of St Peter's Street from Westgate Tower.

"KENT'S BEST"
GEORGE BEER & RIGDEN'S
FAMOUS ALES AND STOUT,
3/4 per crate,   5/6 per doz pints,
3/6 per doz. half pts.

Obtainable at all our Licensed Houses and Bottled Beer Dealers.

Telephone :—No. 258, CANTERBURY.   ::   **No. 91, FAVERSHAM.**

"SERVICE TO MOTORISTS."

We endeavour to give the best service to motorists in the district, and have a **FULLY EQUIPPED MARQUEE ON THESE GROUNDS FOR THE BENEFIT OF ALL.**   Petrol, oil, accessories, tyres, tubes, tools, etc,, are obtainable. Experienced mechanics in attendance.   Punctures repaired and tubes vulcanised while you wait.   ::   **NOTE :—ALL PRICES AS USUAL.**

Stockists and Agents for the following :

TRIUMPH,   ROVER,   OVERLAND,   NEW-HUDSON, RALEIGH, HUMBER, STANDARD, LAGONDA, DOUGLAS Inspect range of all the latest models in our showrooms next to Westgate Towers.

G. R. BARRETT & SON,
Phone : 386,   **THE MOTOR AGENTS,**   **Telegrams :** **(2 lines.)**   **CANTERBURY.**   **Barrett, Motors.**

Established 1858.   Telephone No. 4.   Telegraphic Address—"Coals," Whitstable.
GANN & BROWN, Ltd.,
COAL AND COKE FACTORS AND MERCHANTS,
*Chief Offices—*WHITSTABLE.
Branches at Pluckley, Hythe and Shorncliffe Station for Folkestone, etc.

Prices of all descriptions of Coal on application.   Truck Loads to any Station. Ship Loads to any Harbour.

Any kind of House, Steam, Kitchen, Gas, Cannel and Smith's Coal Supplied. Also Welsh Anthracite for Malting, Hop Drying and Horticultural Purposes. ### SMOKELESS STEAM COAL.
Coke for Household and Foundry use, Small Coal for Engines, Lime Burning and Smiths. Fish Manure & Creosote Merchants.   Shells by the Truck Load to any Station.

LADIES ARE INVITED
to a Free Demonstration by
BOURJOIS — PARIS,
of their renowned
PERFUMES   ::   POWDERS   ::   CREAMS
taking place from
August 5th to August 9th (inclusive) at
FINN'S STORES,   21, ST. MARGARET'S STREET.
(Special Agents)   # CANTERBURY.

The Marquees on this Ground are supplied and erected by G. TWYMAN & SON, Ltd., ST. GEORGE'S PLACE, CANTERBURY. PHONE 22 Enquiries Solicited.

Back of a cricket scorecard from August 1924, advertising local businesses. *(Courtesy of Peggy Poole)*

Index of streets

Other local titles published by Tempus

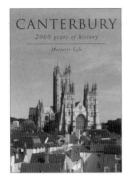

Canterbury: 2000 years of history

MARJORIE LYLE

Making full use of the archaeological discoveries of the last twenty-five years, which have added greatly to our knowledge of Canterbury's two millennia of change, Marjorie Lyle links the city's buildings – the Roman remains, the early Saxon churches, the Norman Cathedral, the pilgrim inns and the medieval timber-framed houses – to the city's history.

0 7524 1948 X

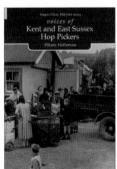

Folklore of Kent

FRAN AND GEOFF DOEL

This book explores the folklore, legends, customs and songs of Kent and their history. From saints to smugglers, hop-pickers to hoodeners, mummers to May garlands, wife sales to witchcraft, this book charts the traditional culture of a culturally significant county.

0 7524 2628 1

Voices of Kent & East Sussex Hop Pickers

HILARY HEFFERNAN

The annual hop-picking season provided a welcome escape for families who lived and worked in the poorer parts of London. The photographs and reminiscences in this book were all provided by people who took part in this traditional migration and their memories tell a fascinating story. They tell of hardship, adventures, mishaps, misfortune and laughter all experienced during hardworking holidays among the bines.

0 7524 3240 0

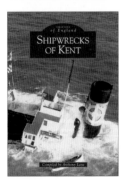

Shipwrecks of Kent

ANTHONY LANE

This compilation of 200 photographs provides a reminder of many of the more famous wrecks, alongside some of the not so familiar disasters from the past, which have occurred over the last two centuries. In addition to ships that got into difficulties, lifeboats and their crews that helped to rescue men have a special place in this pictorial account.

0 7524 1720 7

If you are interested in purchasing other books published by Tempus, or in case you have difficulty finding any Tempus books in your local bookshop, you can also place orders directly through our website

www.tempus-publishing.com